TOURER (GHN 5L)

Driver's Handbook
AKM 3286 MGB (USA)

including

Supplements
AKM 3413 MGB (USA & Canada)
AKM 3404 MGB (USA)

© British Leyland Motor Corporation 1975

FOREWORD

This Handbook provides an introduction to your car, together with information on the care and periodic maintenance required to combine trouble-free motoring with minimal running costs.

Claims for the replacement of parts under warranty must be submitted to the supplying authorized Austin MG Dealer, or when this is not possible, to the nearest authorized Austin MG Dealer, informing them of the vendor's name and address. Except in emergency, warranty work should always be carried out by an appointed authorized Austin MG Dealer.

By keeping the Passport to Service, signed by the authorized Austin MG Dealer, or vendor in the vehicle, you can quickly establish the date of purchase and provide the necessary details if adjustments are required to be carried out under warranty.

Regular use of the Passport to Service Maintenance Scheme is the best safeguard against the possibility of abnormal repair bills at a later date. Failure to have your car correctly maintained could invalidate the terms of the warranty and may result in unsatisfactory operation of the emission control systems.

Safety features embodied in the car may be impaired if other than genuine parts are fitted. In certain territories, legislation prohibits the fitting of parts not to the vehicle manufacturer's specification. Owners purchasing accessories while travelling abroad should ensure that the accessory and its fitted location on the car conform to mandatory requirements existing in their country of origin.

Your authorized Austin MG Dealer is provided with the latest information concerning special service tools and workshop techniques. This enables him to undertake your service and repairs in the most efficient and economic manner. The operations carried out by your authorized Austin MG Dealer will be in accordance with current recommendations and may be subject to revision from time to time.

Further details on service parts will be found under 'SERVICE' on page 69. **Please note that references to right- or left-hand in this Handbook are made as if viewing the car from the rear.**

Specification details set out in this Handbook apply to a range of vehicles and not to any particular vehicle. For the specification of any particular vehicle owners should consult their authorized Austin MG Dealer.

During running-in from new, certain adjustments vary from specification figures detailed. They will be set to specification by your authorized Austin MG Dealer at the After-Sales Service and should be maintained throughout your car's life.

The Manufacturers reserve the right to vary their specifications with or without notice, and at such times and in such manner as they think fit. Major as well as minor changes may be involved in accordance with the Manufacturer's policy of constant product improvement.

Whilst every effort is made to ensure the accuracy of the particulars contained in this Handbook, neither the Manufacturer nor the authorized Austin MG Dealer, by whom this Handbook is supplied, shall in any circumstances be held liable for any inaccuracy or the consequences thereof.

Emission Controls

Your car is fitted with emission controls and devices required by the United States Clean Air Act and the Canadian Federal Motor Vehicle Safety Act.

Please read carefully the 'EMISSION CONTROL SYSTEMS' section of the Handbook which contains information on the emission control systems fitted to your car and recognition of symptoms of malfunctions which could affect emissions.

It is imperative that you familiarize yourself with the contents of this section and ensure that the car you have purchased will remain in compliance with the intentions of the above Acts.

 All maintenance checks and adjustments showing this sign should be entrusted to your authorized Austin MG Dealer.

CONTENTS

Fig. 1 **Synchromesh gearbox**

Pedals
(1) (2) (3)

The pedals are arranged in the conventional positions.

The brake pedal operates the dual hydraulic braking system applying the brakes on all four wheels, also when the ignition is switched on, bringing the stop warning lights into operation.

Gear lever
(4)

The gear positions are indicated on the lever knob. To engage reverse gear move the lever to the left in the neutral position until resistance is felt, apply further side pressure to overcome the resistance and then pull the lever back to engage the gear. The reverse lights operate automatically when reverse is selected with the ignition switched on.

Synchromesh engagement is provided on all forward gears.

Hand brake
(5)

The hand brake is of the pull-up lever type, operating mechanically on the rear wheels only. To release the hand brake pull the lever up slightly, depress the button on the end of the lever and push the lever down.

Fig. 1

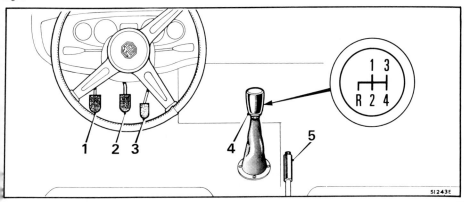

SI243E

WARNING SYSTEMS

Anti-theft warning buzzer A combined ignition and steering lock with warning buzzer is fitted to the car. The warning buzzer will sound if the driver's door is opened while the key is in the lock. The buzzer will not operate if the key is removed from the lock.

When leaving the car unattended always:

Set the hand brake.

Lock the steering by removing the key from the ignition steering lock.

Lock the car doors and remove the key.

Brakes
Fig. 1 **Brake failure warning lamp and test-push switch.** The hydraulic brake system has two independent circuits. If hydraulic pressure fails in one circuit, the remaining circuit will provide an emergency brake condition on the other two wheels and allow the car to be brought to rest by brake pedal application. This would be accompanied by the warning lamp glowing on the instrument panel.

IF THE WARNING LAMP GLOWS AT ANY TIME EXCEPT WHEN THE BULB IS BEING TESTED THE CAUSE MUST BE INVESTIGATED IMMEDIATELY.

Unless as a result of your investigation you are satisfied that it is safe to proceed, you should leave the vehicle where it is and call for assistance. Even if you are satisfied that it is safe to proceed, the car should only be driven in cases of real emergency, extreme care should be taken and heavy braking avoided. In deciding whether it is safe to proceed you should consider whether you will be infringing the law.

To test the warning lamp and circuit, press the switch (1). If the bulb is functioning the light (2) will glow and will go out as the switch is released. To test the hydraulic system, apply normal foot pressure to the brake pedal. The light will remain off if the hydraulic system is functioning satisfactorily. Check the bulb and the system frequently.

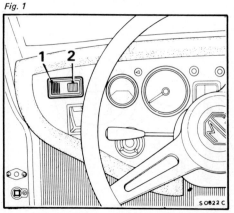

Fig. 1

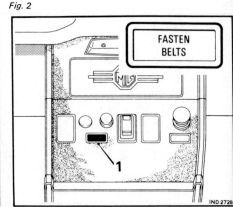

Fig. 2

Seat belt warning
Fig. 2

To ensure that the driver and passenger wear their seat belts when the car is being driven a seat belt warning system is fitted. The system consists of a warning lamp (1) on the control console illuminating the words 'FASTEN BELTS' and a warning buzzer.

The warning system will operate when the ignition starter switch is at position 'III' operating the starter.

See also page 22 for seat belt instructions.

Exhaust gas recirculation (E.G.R.) valve
Fig. 3

The warning lamp (1) for the E.G.R. valve will glow when the car has completed a service interval mileage of approximately 25,000 miles indicating that the E.G.R. valve should be serviced. It is recommended that the E.G.R. valve is serviced by an authorized Austin MG Dealer. An E.G.R. emission service repair kit together with a service interval counter reset key can be purchased from an authorized Austin MG Dealer.

Complete details on servicing the E.G.R. valve are given in Workshop Manual Part No. AKM 3297 obtainable from authorized Austin MG Dealers.

NOTE: As an automatic check the warning lamp will glow each time the ignition key is turned to position 'III' (starter motor operating). Consult your authorized Austin MG Dealer if the lamp fails to glow when the starter is operated.

E.G.R. valve service interval counter
Fig. 3

The service interval counter (2) for the E.G.R. valve is located in the engine compartment and indicates the percentage of service interval mileage that has been completed in a 25,000 mile period.

The counter should be reset to zero immediately after the E.G.R. valve has been serviced.

Fig. 3

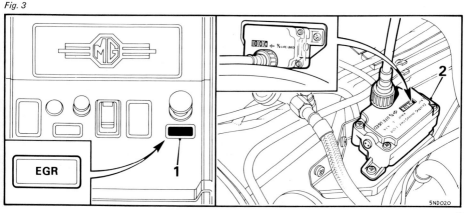

EGR

5ND020

LOCKS

It is most important that owners **MAKE A NOTE OF THE KEY NUMBERS IMMEDIATELY** on taking delivery of the car and at the same time consult their authorized Austin MG Dealer regarding steering lock key replacements.

Keys **Identification.** To reduce the possibility of theft, locks are not marked with a number. Owners are advised to make a note of the numbers stamped on the keys, on the numbered tag supplied, or on a label stuck to the windscreen. The driver and passenger door locks use a common key. The luggage compartment, glovebox and steering locks are operated by separate keys.

Steering The lock face is marked 'O' (off), 'I' (auxiliary), 'II' (ignition), 'III' (start). To
Fig. 1 lock the car steering the key must be removed from the lock (4).

To unlock the steering, insert the key and turn it to position 'I'. If the steering-wheel has been turned to engage the lock, slight movement of the steering-wheel will assist disengagement of the lock plunger.

With the key in the position marked 'I' the ignition is switched off and the steering lock disengaged. The heater blower motor, windscreen wipers/washers, and the radio may be operated with the key in this position. The key must be in this position when towing the car for recovery.

Under no circumstances must the key be moved from the 'I' position towards the 'O' position **WHEN THE CAR IS IN MOTION**. The car may be towed for recovery with the key in the lock at position 'I'.

WARNING.—The lock fitted to the steering-column works in conjunction and is integral with the ignition starter switch. The designed operating sequence prevents the engine being started with the steering LOCKED. **Serious consequences may result from alterations or substitution of the ignition start switch which would permit the engine to be started with the LOCK ENGAGED. Under no circumstances must the ignition switch or the ignition engine start function be separated from the steering lock.**

DO NOT lubricate the steering lock.

Ignition and starter. To switch on the ignition, turn the key to position 'II'. Further movement against spring resistance to position 'III' operates the starter motor. Release the key immediately the engine starts.

Fig. 1

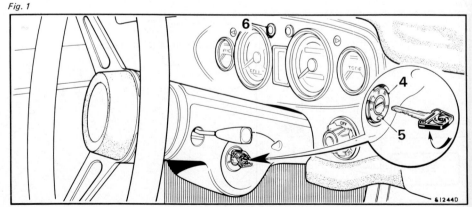

612440

8

The fuel gauge and direction indicators will not operate unless the ignition switch is at position 'II'.

To lock the steering, turn the key anti-clockwise to the position marked 'I', press the button (5), turn the key to the 'O' position and withdraw it.

(6) **Ignition warning light (red).** The ignition warning light serves the dual purpose of reminding the driver to switch off the ignition and of acting as a no-charge indicator. The light should glow when the ignition is switched on, and go out and stay out at all times while the engine is running above normal idling speed.

Door locks
Fig. 2

Both doors may be locked from the outside with the key or from the inside with the internal door handle.

To lock the doors from the outside, turn the key slightly towards the front of the car. To unlock the doors, turn the key slightly towards the rear of the car. After locking or unlocking the doors return the key to the vertical position and withdraw it.

To lock the doors from inside the car, move the locking plate towards the rear of the car (1, inset Fig. 2).

Luggage compartment
Fig. 3

To open, depress the lock plunger and raise the lid. When fully raised the support stay will automatically spring into engagement and the lid will be held in the open position.

To close, raise the lid slightly, push the catch (1) on the bonnet stay forward to release the locking mechanism, and lower the lid. Raising the luggage compartment lid automatically switches on the light.

Glovebox

The glovebox is locked by turning the key anti-clockwise and withdrawing the key from the lock, see page 14.

Fig. 2

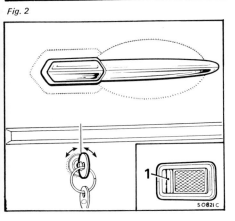

Fig. 3

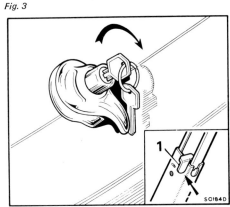

INSTRUMENTS AND SWITCHES

Instruments
Fig. 1

(1) **Speedometer.** In addition to recording the road speed this instrument also records the total distance (3), and the distance travelled for any particular trip (2). To reset the trip recorder, push the knob (4) upwards and turn it clockwise; ensure that all the counters are returned to zero.

(5) **Tachometer.** The instrument indicates the revolutions per minute of the engine and assists the driver to use the most effective engine speed range for maximum performance in any gear.*

(6) **Oil.** The gauge indicates the pressure of the oil in the engine lubrication system.*

(7) **Water.** The gauge is marked 'C' (cold), 'N' (normal), and 'H' (hot), indicating the temperature of the coolant as it leaves the cylinder head.*

(8) **Fuel.** When the ignition is switched on the gauge indicates approximately the amount of fuel in the tank.*

* Also see 'RUNNING INSTRUCTIONS'.

Fig. 1

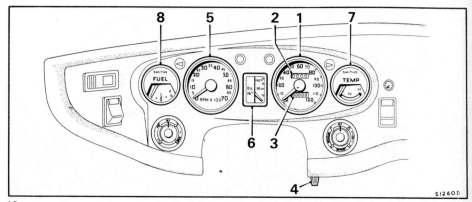

Switches
Fig. 2

(1) **Lighting switch.** Press the lower end of the switch rocker to the first position to operate the parking and tail lamps and to the second position to operate the headlamps. The marking on the switch is illuminated when the panel lamps are switched on.

(2) **Headlamp low beam—(4) Flasher.** With the headlamps switched on at the lighting switch, move the lever down away from the steering-wheel to operate the high beam (3). Lifting the lever towards the steering-wheel from the low-beam position will flash (4) the headlamp high-beams irrespective of whether the lighting switch is on or off.

(5) **Headlamp main-beam warning lamp (blue).** The warning lamp glows when the headlamps are switched on and the beam is in the raised position. The lamp goes out when the beam is lowered.

(6) **Panel lamp switch.** With the parking lamps switched on, illumination of the instruments and switches may be varied by rotating the panel lamp switch knob. Turning the switch knob clockwise from the off position immediately illuminates the panel lamps and further clockwise movement will increase the light brilliance.

Reverse lamps. The reverse lamps operate automatically if reverse gear is selected and the ignition switch is at position 'II' (ignition).

Fig. 2

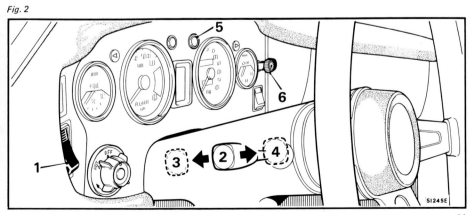

Instruments and Switches

Switches
Fig. 3

(1) **Direction indicators.** The switch is self-cancelling and operates the indicators only when the ignition is switched on. A visual warning of a front or rear bulb failure is given when, after switching on an indicator, the warning lamp and the serviceable bulb on the affected side give a continuous light.

(2) **Direction indicator warning lamps (green).** The arrow-shaped lamps show the direction selected and each operates with the appropriate flashing direction indicators.

(3) **Horn.** The horn is sounded by pressing the centre motif of the steering-wheel.

(4) **Overdrive.** Move the lever towards the steering-wheel to engage overdrive; move the lever away from the steering-wheel to return to direct drive.

(5) **Windscreen wiper.** Move the switch lever down to operate the windscreen wipers at slow speed; further movement in the same direction will operate the wipers at fast speed. The wiper blades park automatically when the switch lever is returned to the off position.

(6) **Windscreen washer.** Press the knob on the end of the switch lever to operate the windscreen washer. When the windscreen is dirty, operate the washer before setting the wipers in motion.

In cold weather the washer reservoir should be filled with a mixture of water and a recommended washer solvent to prevent the water freezing. On no account should radiator anti-freeze or methylated spirits (denatured alcohol) be used in the windscreen washer.

Fig. 3

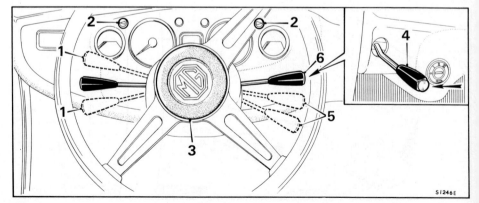

S1246E

Switches
Fig. 4

(1) **Courtesy lamp.** The courtesy lamp is controlled by a switch (2) on the lamp and also by switches operated by the doors. With both doors closed the lamp may be switched on or off using the switch on the lamp. Opening either door switches on the lamp and closing the door extinguishes it.

(4) **Hazard warning.** To use the direction indicators as hazard warning lights, press the lower end of the switch rocker; all direction indicators and the warning lamp (3) will operate together, irrespective of whether the ignition is switched on or off. The marking on the switch is illuminated when the panel lamps are switched on.

(5) **Cigar-lighter.** To operate, press the knob inwards. When ready for use the lighter will partially eject itself and may then be withdrawn. The rim of the cigar-lighter is illuminated when the panel lamps are switched on.

Radio (if fitted). Full operating instructions are supplied with the radio.

Fig. 4

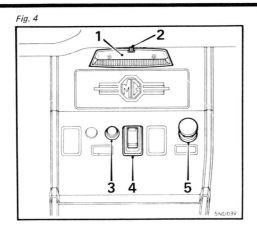

5ND039

BODY FITTINGS

Window regulators
Fig. 1

To open a door window, turn the handle regulator (1) to obtain the opening required.

Front ventilator windows
Fig. 1

To open, move the catch lever (2) upwards and push the window outwards.

To close, pull the catch inwards, and then push it forward until the catch is in the locked position.

Glovebox
Fig. 2

To unlock, insert the key, turn it clockwise, and depress the lock plunger to open the glove box.

To lock, close the glovebox, turn the key anti-clockwise and withdraw the key from the lock.

Bonnet
Fig. 3

To raise the bonnet, pull the knob (1) located inside the car on the left-hand side below the fascia panel.

Press up the safety catch (2) under the front of the bonnet. Raise the bonnet and when fully raised the support stay will automatically spring into engagement and the bonnet will be held in the open position.

To close, raise the bonnet slightly, push the catch (3) on the bonnet stay rearwards to release the locking mechanism, and lower the bonnet. Apply light pressure with the palms of the hands at the front corners of the bonnet and press down quickly; undue force is not necessary and may cause damage. The safety catch and lock will be heard to engage.

Fig. 1

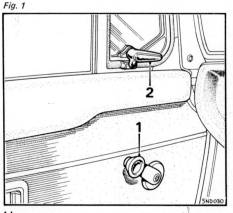

5ND030

Fig. 2

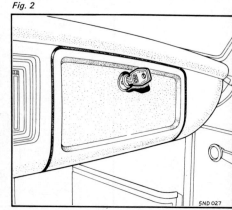

5ND027

Mirrors **External** (Fig. 4). The mirror head may be adjusted from the seat position when the window is open.

Interior (Fig. 5). The mirror stem with anti-dazzle head is designed to break away from the mounting bracket on impact. The stem may be refitted in the mounting bracket as follows. Align the stem ball (1) with the bracket cup (2), ensuring that the small protrusion (3) on the stem aligns with the indent of the mounting bracket. Give them a smart tap with a soft instrument to join the two components.

Anti-dazzle. To reduce mirror dazzle, press the lever (4) towards the windscreen.

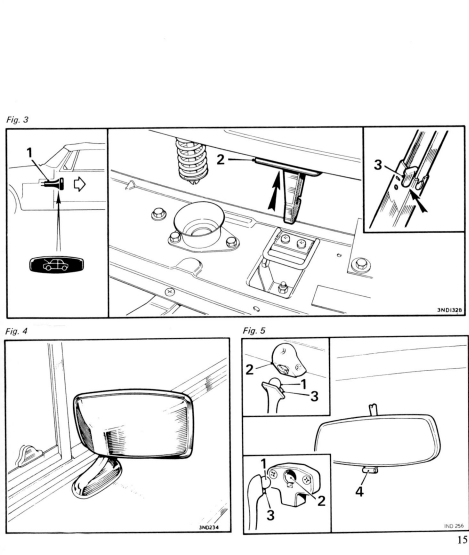

Fig. 3

Fig. 4

Fig. 5

Body Fittings

Arm-rest and ashtray
Fig. 6

To gain access to the compartment below the arm-rest, raise the forward end of the arm-rest. To empty the ashtray, raise the lid (1) and remove the ashtray by lifting under the stubber (2).

Do not attempt to remove the ashtray by pulling on the lid.

Body and door drainage points
Fig. 7

Periodic examination of the drain holes should be made to ensure that they are clear of obstruction; use a piece of stiff wire to probe the apertures.

Careless application of underseal can result in restricted drainage. Masking tape or plugs used when underseal is being applied must be removed immediately the operation is completed.

Jacking up beneath the underfloor may deform the drain apertures; always use the jacking points provided.

Fig. 6

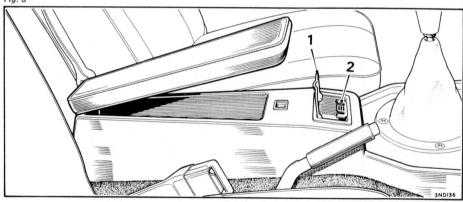

Fig. 7

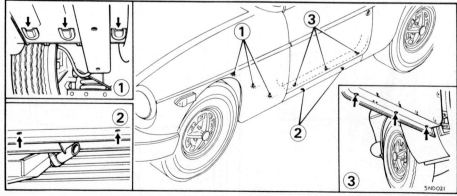

16

Lubrication To ensure trouble-free operation it is essential that the locks, hinges and catches are adequately lubricated.

Locks. Inject a small quantity of thin oil, preferably **Unipart Lockspray,** through the key slots and around the push-buttons. **Do not** oil the steering lock.

Hinges. Apply grease or oil to the joints of the hinges.

Bonnet catches. Apply grease to the moving surfaces of the bonnet release mechanism and oil to the release lever and safety-catch pivot points.

It is most important that the instructions for raising, lowering and folding the hood are followed. Do not fold when the hood is wet or damp.

Lowering the hood Unclip the sun visors (1) and move them to one side.

Fig. 8 Release both windscreen frame toggle catches (2).

Release the two fasteners (3) on the windscreen rails, the two fasteners (4) on the cant rails and the two fasteners (5) on the hood mounting brackets.

Fig. 9 Release the four fasteners from each rear quarter panel (6) and pull the hood slightly forward to disengage the hook (7) from the socket (8) on the body side panel.

Move the seat tilt catch forward and incline the seat backs towards the front of the car.

Fig. 8

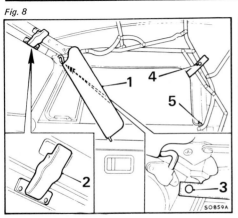

Fig. 9

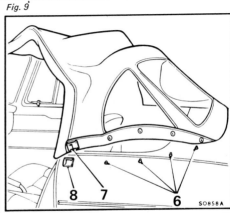

Body Fittings

Fig. 10   Raise the hood header rail (11) until it is poised approximately midway over the door aperture.

Disengage the hood rear rail from the anchor plates (9) on the tonneau panel.

Fold each quarter-light (10) onto the back-light and continue the fold in the material forward to the header rail (11). **ENSURE THAT THE FOLD IS MADE IN THE HOOD MATERIAL BETWEEN THE QUARTER-LIGHT AND THE BACK-LIGHT. FAILURE TO DO THIS MAY CAUSE PERMANENT DAMAGE TO THE BACK-LIGHT MATERIAL.**

Push the header rail (11) rearwards, and at the same time draw the back-light and hood material (12) out over the luggage compartment lid ensuring that the hood material does not become trapped between the hood sticks.

Fig. 11   Fully lower the hood. Fold the two windscreen frame toggle catches (13) rearwards to prevent them damaging the back-light.

Roll the back-light and material forward over the folded hood. Position and secure the two retaining straps (14).

Replace the sun visors and return the seat back-rests to their original positions.

Raising the hood
Fig. 8, Fig. 9 and Fig. 10

Remove the hood cover. Move the seat tilt catch forwards and incline the seat backs towards the front of the car.

Unclip the sun visors (1) and move to one side.

Raise the header rail (11) and unfold the hood. Engage the rear rail in the anchor plates (9). Pull the hood slightly forwards and engage each hook (7) in its socket (8) on the body side panel. Position the header rail on the windscreen ensuring the rail seal is forward of the seal flange. Secure the windscreen frame toggle catches and fasteners (3), (4), and (5) inside the car.

Secure the fasteners (6) at each rear quarter.

Reposition the seats and sun visors.

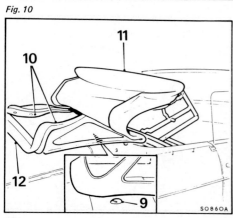

Fig. 10

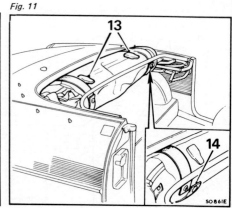

Fig. 11

18

Fitting the hood cover
Figs. 12 and 13

Assemble the hood cover rail (15) and fit it into the hood support sockets with the cross-rod towards the rear.

Lay the hood over the rail.

Engage the cover rear rail in the two anchor plates (16) on the tonneau panel.

Pull the cover slightly forwards and engage each side hook in its socket (17) on the body panel.

Secure the fasteners (18) at each quarter side panel.

Secure the four fasteners (19) inside the car.

Removing the hood cover

Reverse the fitting procedure.

Stowage

Stowage bags are provided to protect the hood cover and hood cover rail. The stowage bags together with the tool bag are stowed in the luggage compartment and secured with the straps provided.

Fig. 12

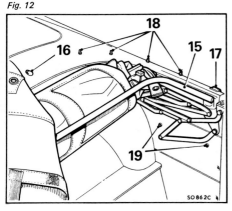

SO862C

Fig. 13

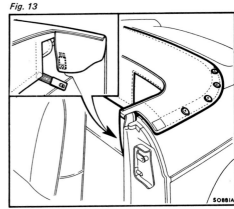

SO88IA

Body Fittings

Hard top **Fitting.** Remove the hood. Fit the hard top side brackets into the hood support sockets and secure with the bolts and spring washers.

Position the hard top on the car, engaging the rear securing plates with the slotted anchor plates on the tonneau panel (inset, Fig. 14) ensuring that the sealing rubber does not foul the slots.

Line up the hard top drip moulding with the rear wing top beading. Push the hard top forwards and engage the toggle catch tongues in the sockets on the windscreen frame.

Fit the bolts into the side fixing brackets; screw in but do not tighten. Ensure that the front sealing rubber is correctly positioned forward of the windscreen frame. Adjust the toggle catches to give adequate tension (when fastened the securing bolt slots allow movement), tighten the securing bolts, fasten the catches and lock them with the securing clips (inset, Fig. 15).

Check that the sealing rubbers are correctly positioned, then slowly and evenly tighten the side fixing bolts until the hard top seals evenly to the body. **AVOID OVERTIGHTENING.** Measure the gap between the hard top and body side fixing brackets (arrowed, Fig. 14). Remove the bolts and fit washers between the brackets to the thickness of the gap. Refit and tighten the bolts.

Wind up both windows and check that a gap of approximately $\frac{5}{16}$ in. exists between the rear edge of the window and the hard top quarter channel. Adjust if necessary by loosening the side fixing bolts and repositioning the hard top. Ensure that there is an adequate seal between the window and hard top rubber and that the doors, when opened with the windows up, do not foul the opening surround.

Removing. Unlock and release the windscreen toggle fasteners. Remove the side fixing bolts. Raise the front of the hard top to disengage the toggle fastener tongues from the windscreen sockets, move the hard top to the rear to disengage the anchor plates, then lift it clear of the car. Remove the side fixing brackets from the hood support sockets. Assemble the fittings loosely to the hard top to prevent loss.

Fig. 14

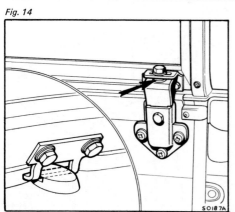

S0187A

Fig. 15

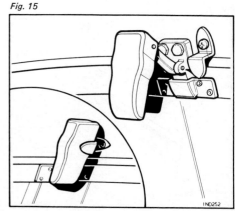

IND252

Tonneau cover
Fig. 16

Fitting. Lay the tonneau cover over the cockpit and place the pockets in the cover over the head restraints on the seats.

Engage the rear edge retainer with the slotted plates on the tonneau panel, and secure to each quarter panel with the fasteners.

Extend the tonneau cover forward and attach the front of the cover to the fasteners on the fascia panel top and windscreen pillars.

Fig. 17   **Usage.** The centre zip allows the cover to be folded down to give access to the driving seat or to both seats. Fold the cover down behind the seat and secure it with the fasteners on the flap to the heelboard.

The short side zips allow the seat belt to be used.

Removing. Reverse the fitting procedure.

Fig. 16

Fig. 17

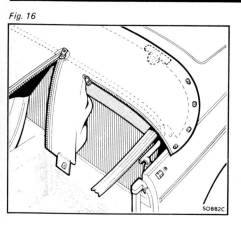

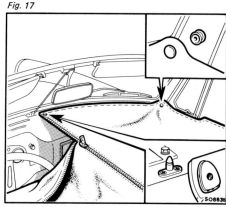

SEATS AND SEAT BELTS

SEATS *Fig. 1*

Adjustment Both seats are adjustable and can be moved easily into the most comfortable position. To adjust either seat, move the lever (1) located beneath the front of the seat outwards; hold the lever in this position while the seat position is adjusted. The locking pin will automatically lock the seat in the required position when the lever is released. To adjust the rake of the back of the seat, ease the body weight from the seat back, move the lever (2) in the direction of the arrow. Release the lever and ensure the seat back is fully locked in position; check by applying back pressure on the seat.

To gain access to the rear compartment, move the seat tilt catch (3) forward, and fold the back of the seat against the steering-wheel. The tilt catch will automatically re-engage when the rear of the seat is moved back to the correct driving position.

Head restraint The head restraint (4) may be raised or lowered as desired.

SEAT BELTS *Fig. 2*

Warning System The seat belt warning system functions when the ignition/starter switch is operated. Two types of system are fitted.

First type. The buzzer will sound and the **'FASTEN BELT'** lamp will be switched on if the ignition/starter switch is operated before the seat belt of each occupied front seat is fastened. **DO NOT** travel with a heavy parcel on the passenger seat.

The **'FASTEN BELTS'** warning lamp and buzzer will not operate if the following simple sequence is carried out at all times.

1. Sit in the seat.
2. Wear and fasten the seat belt.

A front seat passenger must follow the same sequence.

Second type. The **'FASTEN BELTS'** lamp will be switched on for eight seconds each time the ignition/starter switch is operated. The warning buzzer will sound for eight seconds if the ignition/starter switch is operated before the driver's seat belt is fastened.

Fig. 1

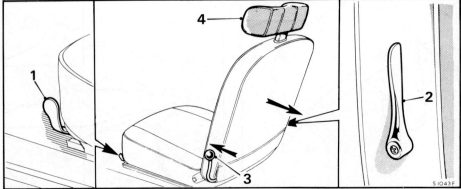

S 1043 F

| **To fasten** | Lift the engagement tongue (1) and draw the belt from the automatic reel over the shoulder and across the chest, and push it into the locking clip (2) of the short belt nearest the wearer. |

To release Press the release button (3) on the short belt.

To stow Place the engagement tongue (1) into the stowing pocket (5) mounted under the hood centre locating socket.

Wearing Never attempt to wear the belt other than as a complete diagonal and lap assembly. Do not try to use the belt for more than one person at any one time, even children.

Testing WARNING.—This test must be carried out under safe road conditions, i.e. on a dry, straight, metalled road, during a period when the road is free from traffic. With the belts in use, drive the car at 5 m.p.h. (8 km.p.h.) and brake sharply. The automatic locking device should operate and lock the belt. It is essential that the driver and passenger are sitting in a normal relaxed position when making the test. The retarding effect of the braking must not be anticipated.

If a belt fails to lock, consult your authorized Austin MG Dealer.

Care of the belts No unauthorized alterations or additions to the belts should be made. Do not bleach or re-dye the belt webbing. Inspect the webbing periodically for signs of abrasion, cuts, fraying, and general wear; pay particular attention to the fixing points and adjusters. Replace belts that are defective or have been subjected to severe strain.

After releasing the belt, allow the webbing to retract into the automatic reel. Ensure that while the belt is retracted the engagement tongue (1) has not moved on the belt to a point near the sill mounting; this can be remedied by moving the tongue and belt clip (4) towards the reel.

Do not attempt to bleach the belt webbing or re-dye it. If the belts become soiled, sponge with warm water using a non-detergent soap and allow to dry naturally.

Do not use caustic soap, chemical cleaners or detergents for cleaning: do not dry with artificial heat or by direct exposure to the sun.

Fig. 2

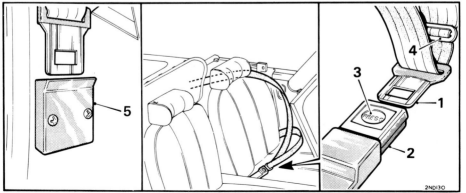

2ND130

HEATING AND VENTILATING

Fresh air Fresh air is admitted to the car for cooling and ventilation through an adjustable
Fig. 1 vent mounted behind the centre console.

Air enters the car interior through the two doors located one each side of the
gearbox tunnel in the foot wells.

The flow of air may be adjusted by moving the control knob (1) backwards to
one of the three open positions; move the knob to the most forward position to
close the vent.

Face-level Air flow for cooling and ventilation from the face-level vents mounted on the
vents fascia panel may be adjusted by turning the serrated control wheels (2) to open
Fig. 1 the vents.

The direction of the air flow is adjusted by moving the shutter control knob (3)
mounted in the centre of each vent.

Fresh-air The heating and ventilating system is designed to provide fresh air either heated
heater by the engine cooling system or at outside temperature to the car at floor level
and for demisting and defrosting to the windscreen. Full heat output is not
available until the engine has reached normal operating temperature.

Air distribution for heating is independent of the fresh-air system; the control
knob (1) (in Fig. 1) should be in the closed position when heated air is being
distributed.

Fig. 1

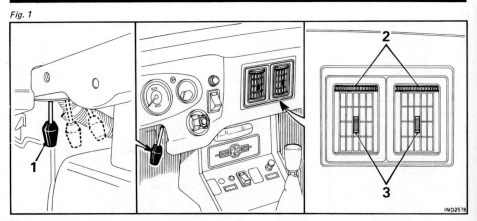

IND2578

Heater controls
Fig. 2

Air temperature. Turn the knob (1) in the direction of the arrow to raise the air temperature.

Air flow. Turn the knob (2) in the direction of the arrow to direct the air distribution.

Booster. Press the lower end of the switch rocker (3) to boost the air flow.

Use the booster when the car is stationary, moving at a slow speed, or to augment the air supply in adverse weather conditions.

Usage The heater and air flow controls may be set at the position marked on the control knobs or to any other intermediate positions. By varying the control settings, and utilizing the booster blower, a wide range of settings can be obtained to suit prevailing conditions.

Illumination The markings on the booster switch and the control dials and the position indicators on the rotary control knobs are illuminated when the panel lamps are switched on.

Fig. 2

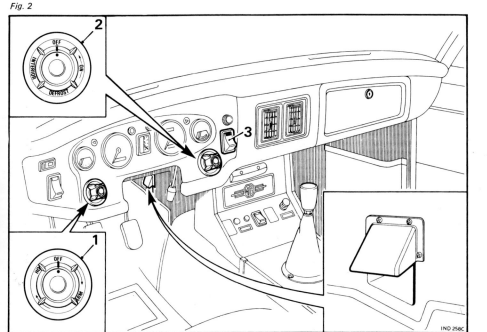

IND 258C

25

RUNNING INSTRUCTIONS

The following instructions are a guide for starting, running and loading the car, and include notes on the use of the controls and the indications of the instruments.

WARNING: Exhaust fumes will be drawn into the car if it is driven with the boot lid open, causing a health hazard to the passenger and driver.

If it is imperative that the car be driven with the boot lid open, adverse effects can be minimized by adopting the following procedure:

1. Close all windows.
2. Open the face vents fully.
3. Set the heater controls to circulate the maximum amount of cold or hot air.
4. Switch on the blower motor.
5. Do not travel at high speed.

Change of fuel
The engine has been designed to operate on 'Regular' fuel and has not been developed for the regular use of unleaded or low lead fuels. The use of such fuels cannot be recommended as they could have a detrimental effect on engine components, resulting in loss of performance, excess exhaust emissions and, possibly, complete engine failure.

Starting
Sit in the car, then wear and fasten the seat belts; this applies to both driver and passenger.

Switch on the ignition and check:
 That the ignition warning light glows.
 That the fuel gauge registers.

Depress the throttle pedal fully and release.

Operate the starter. Do not depress the throttle pedal while the starter is operated.

As soon as the engine is started check:
 That the oil pressure gauge registers.
 The ignition warning light has gone out.

Within thirty seconds of starting the engine, quickly depress and release the throttle pedal to set the automatic choke to its correct position.

Induction chamber heater
Fig. 1
An induction chamber heater is fitted and operates below 4°C (40°F). When starting below this temperature it is necessary to allow a warming up period of thirty seconds between switching on the ignition and starting the engine.

Never leave the ignition switched on in excess of the recommended periods with the engine at rest.

Fuel pump inertia switch
Fig. 2
The electrical supply to the fuel pump is switched off by an inertia switch if the car is subjected to a moderate impact. The switch (1), shown in the off position, is located under the fascia on the left-hand side. To reset the switch unscrew the three screws (2) to release the bottom panel (3) push the plunger (4) into the switch body and refit the bottom panel.

Ignition warning lamp
The lamp should glow when the engine is switched on, and go out and stay out at all times when the engine is running above normal idling speed. Failure to do so indicates a fault in the battery charging system. Check that the fan belt is correctly tensioned before consulting your authorized Austin MG Dealer.

Starter   Do not operate the starter for longer than five to six seconds.

To prevent damage the starter cannot be operated while the engine is running. If the engine fails to start, the ignition key must be returned to the off position before the starter can be operated again.

If after a reasonable number of attempts the engine should fail to start, switch off the ignition and investigate the cause. Continued use of the starter when the engine will not start not only discharges the battery but may also damage the starter.

Oil pressure gauge   The gauge should register a pressure as soon as the engine is started up. The pressure may rise above 80 lb./sq. in. when the engine is started from cold, and as the oil is circulated and warmed the pressure should then drop to between 50 and 80 lb./sq. in. at normal running speeds and to between 10 and 25 lb./sq. in. at idling speed.

Should the gauge fail to register any pressure, stop the engine immediately and investigate the cause. Start by checking the oil level.

Temperature gauge   Normal operating temperature is reached when the pointer is in the 'N' sector.

Overheating may cause serious damage. Investigate any upward change in the temperature gauge reading immediately. Check coolant level and fan belt tension.

When the ignition is switched off the needle returns to the 'cold' position.

Tachometer   For normal road work, and to obtain the most satisfactory service from your engine, select the appropriate gear to maintain engine speeds of between 2,000 and 4,500 r.p.m.

When maximum acceleration is required upward gear selections should be made when the needle reaches the yellow sector (5,500–6,000 r.p.m.). Prolonged or excessive use of the highest engine speeds will tend to shorten the life of the engine. Allowing the engine to pull hard at low engine speeds must be avoided as this also has a detrimental effect on the engine.

The beginning of the red sector (6,000 r.p.m.) indicates the maximum safe speed for the engine.

Never allow the needle to enter the red sector.

Fig. 1

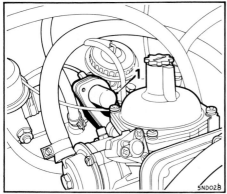

5ND02B

Fig. 2

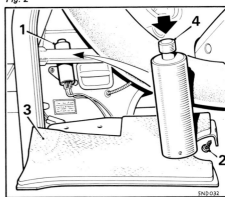

5ND032

Running Instructions

Running in   The treatment given to a new car will have an important bearing on its subsequent life, and engine speeds during this early period must be limited. The following instructions should be strictly adhered to.

During the first 500 miles:

DO NOT exceed 45 m.p.h.

DO NOT operate at full throttle in any gear.

DO NOT allow the engine to labour in any gear.

Wet brakes   If the car has been washed, driven through water, or over wet roads for prolonged periods full braking power may not be available. Dry the brakes by applying the foot brake lightly several times while the car is in motion. Keep the hand brake applied while using high-pressure washing equipment.

Vehicle loading   Due consideration must be given to the overall weight carried when fully loading the car. Any loads carried on a luggage rack or downward load from a towing hitch must also be included in the maximum loading.

Towing   **The towing weight of 1,680 lb. is the maximum that is permissible.** When using bottom gear a gradient of up to 1 in 8 can be ascended while towing a weight not exceeding this figure. It may be necessary to adjust the maximum towing weight to comply with local conditions and regulations. The recommended downward load of a trailer or caravan on the towing hitch is 75 to 100 lb., but this may be reduced or exceeded at the discretion of the driver. Any load carried on the roof or downward load from a towing hitch must also be included in the maximum loading of the vehicle.

Towing for recovery   Should it become necessary to tow the car, use the towing-eyes provided.

For recovery the car should be towed with the key in the ignition/steering lock at position 'I'. For tow starting the key should be at position 'II'.

Overdrive (if fitted)   The overdrive unit, controlled by a switch on the steering-column, provides a higher driving ratio, for use with third or fourth gear. To engage overdrive move the switch lever towards the steering-wheel; to disengage move the lever away from the steering-wheel. Accelerator pedal pressure should be maintained and it is not necessary to depress the clutch pedal during engagement or disengagement.

Overdrive can be engaged at any throttle opening when in third or top gear. If increased acceleration is required the overdrive can be 'switched out' without alteration to the throttle setting. Do not 'switch out' the overdrive when travelling at speeds exceeding normal third or top gear road speeds.

In certain driving conditions while travelling in third gear, the overdrive can be switched in to provide a top gear ratio or out to provide third gear acceleration without the necessity of manually moving the gear-change lever.

If for any reason the overdrive does not disengage, do not reverse the car otherwise extensive damage may result.

CLEANING

Interior　**Carpets:** Clean with a semi-stiff brush or a vacuum cleaner, preferably before washing the outside of the car. Occasionally give the carpets a thorough cleaning with a suitable upholstery cleaner. Carpets must not be 'dry-cleaned'.

Plastic faced upholstery: Clean with diluted upholstery cleaner. Spot clean with upholstery cleaner spread thinly over the surface with a brush or cloth, leave for five minutes, then wipe over with a damp sponge or cloth.

Nylon faced upholstery: Remove loose dirt with a brush or vacuum cleaner. The nylon pile has been chemically treated to resist soiling and care must be taken when cleaning. To remove a stain, apply a nylon cleaner, then pat and wipe with a clean cloth in the direction of the pile until the stain is removed. **DO NOT RUB.** When dry, gently brush against the pile, then with the pile.

Body　Regular care of the body finish is necessary if the new appearance of the car exterior is to be maintained against the effects of air pollution, rain, and mud.

Wash the bodywork frequently, using a soft sponge and plenty of water containing car shampoo. Large deposits of mud must be softened with water before using the sponge. Smears should be removed by a second wash in clean water, and with the sponge if necessary. When dry, clean the surface of the car with a damp chamois-leather. In addition to the regular maintenance, special attention is required if the car is driven in extreme conditions such as sea spray or on salted roads. In these conditions and with other forms of severe contamination an additional washing operation is necessary which should include underbody hosing. Any damaged areas should be immediately covered with paint and a complete repair effected as soon as possible. Before touching-in light scratches and abrasions with paint, thoroughly clean the surface. Use petrol/white spirit (gasoline/hydrocarbon solvent) to remove spots of grease or tar.

Bright trim　Never use an abrasive on stainless, chromium, aluminium, or plastic bright parts and on no account clean them with metal polish. Remove spots of grease or tar with petrol/white spirit (gasoline/hydrocarbon solvent) and wash frequently with water containing car shampoo. When the dirt has been removed polish with a clean dry cloth or chamois-leather until bright. Any slight tarnish found on stainless or plated components which have not received regular attention may be removed with chrome cleaner. An occasional application of light mineral oil or grease will help to preserve the finish, particularly during winter when salt may be used on the roads, but these protectives must not be applied to plastic finishes.

COOLING SYSTEM

Radiator filler cap
Fig. 1
(1)

The system is pressurized to 10 lb./sq. in. when hot, and the pressure must be released gradually when the filler cap is removed. It is advisable to protect the hands against escaping steam and turn the cap slowly anti-clockwise until the resistance of the safety stops is felt. Leave the cap in this position until all pressure is released. Press the cap downwards against the spring to clear the safety stops, and continue turning until it can be lifted off.

Draining the cooling system

To drain the cooling system, slacken the hose clip and remove the bottom hose at its connection to the radiator. Remove the drain plug (2) on the engine cylinder block.

When draining in freezing weather, do so when the engine is hot. Run the engine slowly for one minute when the water has ceased flowing to clear any water from the pump and other places where it might collect. Finally, leave a reminder on the vehicle to the effect that the cooling system has been drained.

Collect the coolant in a clean container if it is to be used again, as cars are filled with a 50% solution of anti-freeze before they leave the factory.

Filling the cooling system

To avoid wastage by overflow add just sufficient coolant to cover the bottom of the header tank. Run the engine until it is hot and add sufficient coolant to bring the surface to the level of the indicator positioned inside the header tank below the filler neck.

NOTE.—The heater control must be set to 'HOT' when draining or filling the cooling system.

Fig. 1

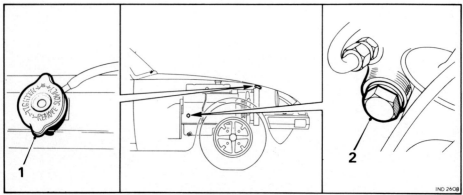

IND 2608

Frost precautions Water expands when it freezes, and if precautions are not taken there is considerable risk of bursting the radiator, cylinder block, or heater. Such damage may be avoided by adding anti-freeze to the water.

Do not use radiator anti-freeze solution in the windscreen washer.

Anti-freeze solutions Anti-freeze can remain in the cooling system for two years provided that the specific gravity of the coolant is checked periodically and anti-freeze added as necessary. The specific gravity check should be carried out by an authorized Austin MG Dealer.

Top up only when the cooling system is at its normal running temperature in order to avoid losing anti-freeze due to expansion.

After the second winter the system should be drained and flushed. Refer to the instructions given for draining the cooling system, then clean out the system thoroughly by flushing water through the radiator passages using a hose inserted in the radiator filler orifice.

Before adding the recommended anti-freeze make sure that the cooling system is watertight; examine all joints and replace any defective hose with new.

We recommend owners to use **anti-freeze** with an ethlyene glycol base which conforms to specification S.A.E. J1034, or B.S.3151/2 to protect the cooling system during frosty weather and reduce corrosion to the minimum.

The correct quantities of anti-freeze for different degrees of frost protection are:

Anti-freeze	Commences to freeze		Frozen solid		Amount of anti-freeze
%	°C.	°F.	°C.	°F.	U.S. Pts.
25	−13	9	−26	−15	3
33⅓	−19	− 2	−36	−33	4
50	−36	−33	−48	−53	6

WHEELS AND TYRES

Jacking up
Fig. 1

The jack is designed to lift one side of the car at a time. Apply the hand brake, and block the wheels on the opposite side to that being jacked; use a wood block jammed tight against the tyre tread.

Insert the lifting arm of the jack into the socket located in the door sill panel. **Make certain that the jack lifting arm is pushed fully into the socket and that the base of the jack is on firm ground.** The jack should lean slightly outwards at the top to allow for the radial movement of the car as it is raised.

WARNING.—Do not work beneath the vehicle with the lifting jack as the sole means of support. Place suitable supports under the front side-members or rear axle to give adequate support and safety while working.

Jack maintenance

If the jack is neglected it may be difficult to use in a roadside emergency. Examine it occasionally, clean off accumulated dust, and lightly oil the thread to prevent the formation of rust.

WHEELS
Preventive maintenance

Owners are recommended to check wheel nuts for tightness each week in addition to checking the other items listed. Take care not to overtighten (torque wrench setting 60 to 65 lb. ft.).

Pressed type
Removing and refitting
Fig. 2

Slacken the four nuts securing the road wheel to the hub; turn anti-clockwise to loosen and clockwise to tighten. Raise the car with the jack to lift the wheel clear of the ground and remove the nuts. Withdraw the road wheel from the hub.

When refitting the road wheel locate the wheel on the hub, lightly tighten the nuts (1) with the wheel nut spanner (securing nuts must be fitted with the **taper side towards the wheel**), and lower the jack. Fully tighten the wheel nuts, tightening them diagonally and progressively, at the same time avoid over-tightening.

The wheel centre trim (2) must be removed and fitted to the wheel in use.

Replace the wheel disc and jack socket plug.

Fig. 1

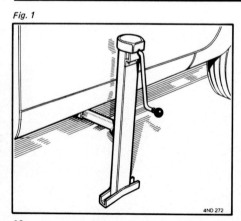

Fig. 2

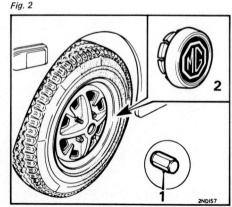

Wire type (if fitted)

Removing and refitting Fig. 3

Use the spanner and hammer to slacken and tighten the octagonal hub nuts.

Always jack up a wheel before using the tools, and always tighten the hub nuts fully.

Hub nuts are marked 'LEFT' or 'RIGHT' to show which side of the car they must be fitted, and also with the word 'UNDO' and an arrow.

Before replacing a wheel wipe all serrations, threads, and cones of the wheel and hub and then lightly coat them with grease. If a forced change is made on the road, remove, clean, and grease as soon as convenient.

Maintenance

When the car is new, after the first long run or after 50 miles of short runs, jack up the wheels and use the hammer and spanner to make sure that the nuts are tight.

Spare wheel

Fig. 4

The spare wheel is stowed in the well of the luggage compartment.

Unscrew the clamp plate (1) to release the spare wheel.

When refitting, position the wheel face down in the well of the luggage compartment and retain in position with the clamp plate.

The spare wheel tyre on new cars is inflated above the recommended running pressure. The pressure must be checked and adjusted before use.

Fig. 3

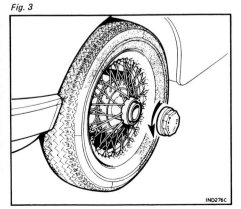

IND276C

Fig. 4

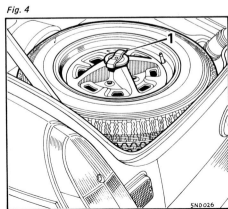

5ND026

Wheels and Tyres

TYRES

Markings Tyres are marked with the maximum load and inflation pressure figures. When fitting replacement tyres ensure that they are to the same specification and marking. **The permissible load and tyre pressures are shown on pages 67 and 68 of this handbook.**

Wear indicator Tyres fitted as original equipment have wear indicators incorporated in their tread pattern. When the tyre tread has worn down until 0·06 in. of the tread is remaining the wear indicator bar will appear across the full width of the tread pattern.

Maintenance Tyres, including the spare, must be maintained at the pressures recommended (see 'GENERAL DATA'); check with an accurate tyre gauge at least once a week, and regulate as necessary. Pressures should be checked when the tyres are cold; do not reduce the pressure in warm tyres where the increase above the normal pressure is due to temperature. See that the valve caps are screwed down firmly by hand. The cap prevents the entry of dirt into the valve mechanism and forms an additional seal on the valve, preventing any leakage if the valve core is damaged. The spare wheel supplied with new cars is inflated above the recommended running pressure. The pressure must be checked and adjusted before use.

Excessive local distortion can cause the casing of a tyre to fracture and may lead to premature tyre failure. Tyres should be examined, especially for cracked walls, exposed cords, etc. Flints and other sharp objects should be removed from the tyre tread; if neglected, they may work through the cover. Any oil or grease which may get onto the tyres should be cleaned off by using fuel sparingly. Do not use paraffin (kerosene), which has a detrimental effect on rubber.

Repairs When repairing tubes, have punctures or injuries vulcanized. Ordinary patches should only be used for emergencies. Vulcanizing is absolutely essential for tubes manufactured from synthetic rubber.

Replacement Radial-ply tyres are standard equipment and **replacements must be of the radial-ply type.**

Wheel and tyre balancing Unbalanced wheel and tyre assemblies may be responsible for abnormal wear of the tyres and vibration in the steering. Consult your authorized Austin MG Dealer.

BRAKES

Front brake pads
Fig. 1

Wear on the disc brake friction pads (arrowed) is automatically compensated for during braking operations and manual adjustment is therefore not required.

If the wear on one pad is greater than on the other their operating positions should be changed over by your authorized Austin MG Dealer.

Remove the road wheel to gain clear access to the pads for inspection.

The pads must be renewed when the lining material has worn to the minimum permissible thickness of $\frac{1}{16}$ in. (1.6 mm.) or will have done so before the next regular inspection is due. Special equipment is required to renew the brake pads; this work should be entrusted to your authorized Austin MG Dealer.

After fitting new pads, within the limits of safety, heavy braking should be avoided for a few days to allow the pads to bed-in.

Rear brakes
Fig. 2

Excessive brake pedal travel is an indication that the rear brake-shoes require adjusting. The brake-shoes on both rear wheels must be adjusted to regain even and efficient braking.

Adjusting. Chock the front wheels, fully release the hand brake and jack up each rear wheel in turn, placing suitable supports beneath the vehicle—see **'WARNING'** on page 32. Turn the adjuster (1) in a clockwise direction (viewed from the centre of the car), using a **Brake Adjusting Spanner** until the brake-shoes lock the wheel, then turn the adjuster back until the wheel is free to rotate without the shoes rubbing. Repeat the adjustment on the other rear brake.

Hand brake
Fig. 2

The hand brake is automatically adjusted with the rear brakes. If there is excessive movement of the hand brake lever, consult your authorized Austin MG Dealer. To lubricate, charge the nipple (2) on the hand brake cable with one of the recommended greases.

Fig. 1

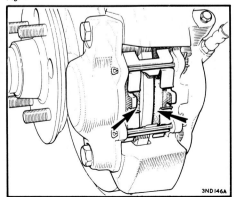

3ND146A

Fig. 2

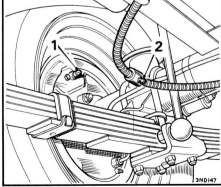

3ND147

Brakes

Replacing brake-shoes or pads

When it becomes necessary to renew brake-shoes or pads it is essential that only genuine replacements, with the correct grade of lining, are used. Always fit new shoes or pads as complete axle sets, never individually or as a single wheel set. Serious consequences could result from out-of-balance braking due to mixing of linings.

Replacement brake-shoes or pads are obtainable from your authorized Austin MG Dealer.

Inspecting rear brake linings
Fig. 3

Chock the front wheels and release the hand brake. Jack up each rear wheel in turn, placing suitable supports beneath the vehicle—see **'WARNING'** on page 32.

Remove the road wheel and slacken the brake-shoe adjuster fully.

Remove the two countersunk screws (1) and withdraw the brake-drum (2).

Inspect the linings (3) for wear, and clean the dust from the backplate assembly and drum, preferably using methylated spirit (denatured alcohol). Brake lining dust is dangerous to health if inhaled and therefore should not be blown from the drums. Make certain that sufficient lining material remains to allow the car to run until the next regular inspection is due without the thickness falling below the safe limit.

Refit the brake drums and the road wheels and adjust the brake-shoes (see page 35).

Fig. 3

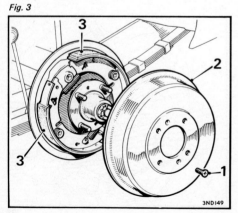

Fig. 4

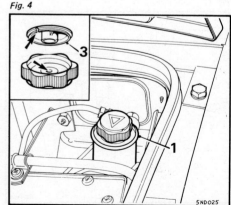

Brake and clutch master cylinder
Figs. 4 and 5

To check the level of the fluid in the clutch master cylinder reservoir (1), remove the plastic filler cap. The fluid level must be maintained at the bottom of the filler neck.

The level of the fluid in the brake master cylinder reservoir is visible through the plastic reservoir (2); the level must be maintained up to the bottom of the filler neck.

Use only **Lockheed Disc Brake Fluid (Series 329S)** or **Castrol Girling Brake Fluid**; alternatively, use a brake fluid conforming to **F.M.V. S.S. D.O.T.3 specification with a minimum boiling-point of 260°C (500°F).**

Before refitting the filler caps, separate the dome (3) from the filler cap and check that the breather holes, indicated by arrows, are clear. Snap fit the dome onto the filler cap.

NOTE.—Brake fluid can have a detrimental effect on paintwork. Ensure that fluid is not allowed to contact paint-finished surfaces.

Brake servo

Filter renewing. The filter is located in the servo housing where the push-rod passes through from the brake pedal. Renewing of the filter should be entrusted to your authorized Austin MG Dealer.

Fig. 5

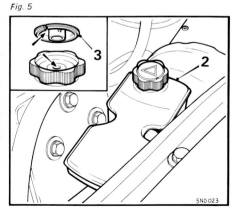

Fig. 6

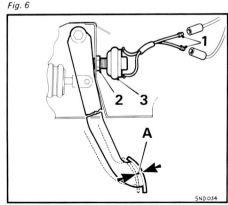

Brakes

Brake pedal
Fig. 6
A free movement of $\frac{1}{8}$ in. (A), measured at the pedal pad must be maintained on the pedal. To adjust the free movement, disconnect the stop light switch wiring (1), slacken the locknut (2), and turn the switch (3) clockwise to decrease or anti-clockwise to increase the clearance. Tighten the stop light switch locknut and connect the wiring.

Preventive maintenance
In addition to the recommended periodical inspection of brake components it is advisable as the car ages, and as a precaution against the effects of wear and deterioration, to make a more searching inspection and renew parts as necessary.

It is recommended that:

(1) Disc brake pads, drum brake linings, hoses, and pipes should be examined at intervals no greater than those laid down in the Maintenance Summary.

(2) Brake fluid should be changed completely every 18 months or 19,000 miles whichever is the sooner.

(3) All fluid seals and all flexible hoses in the hydraulic system should be renewed every 3 years or 37,500 miles whichever is the sooner. At the same time the working surface of the piston and of the bores of the master cylinders, wheel cylinders, and other slave cylinders should be examined and new parts fitted where necessary.

Care must be taken always to observe the following points:

(*a*) At all times use the recommended brake fluid.

(*b*) Never leave fluid in unsealed containers. It absorbs moisture quickly and this can be dangerous.

(*c*) Fluid drained from the system or used for bleeding is best discarded.

(*d*) The necessity for absolute cleanliness throughout cannot be over-emphasized.

ELECTRICAL

POLARITY   The electrical installation on this car is **NEGATIVE** ($-$) earth return and the correct polarity must be maintained at all times. Reversed polarity will permanently damage semi-conductor devices in the alternator and tachometer, and the radio transistors (when fitted). Never use an ohmmeter of the type incorporating a hand-driven generator for checking semi-conductor components.

Before fitting a radio or any other electrical equipment, make certain that it has the correct polarity for installation in this vehicle.

BATTERY
Access
Fig. 1

Release the rear seat cushion securing straps from the fasteners, and pull the cushion forward.

Remove the carpet covering the rear compartment floor. Turn the three quick-release fasteners (1) anti-clockwise one half turn and remove the battery compartment cover panel (2).

Checking
topping-up
Fig. 1

The vehicle must be on level ground when the electrolyte is being checked.

DO NOT USE A NAKED LIGHT WHEN CHECKING THE LEVELS and do not use tap water for topping-up.

Remove the battery vent cover; use the grip at the centre of the cover (3), this will ensure that the filling valves are operated correctly. If no electrolyte is visible inside the battery, pour distilled water into the filling trough until the six tubes (4), and the connecting trough (5), are filled. Refit the vent cover.

The above operations should not be carried out within half an hour of the battery having been charged, other than by the vehicle's own generating system, lest it floods. In extremely cold conditions run the engine immediately after topping-up so as to mix the electrolyte.

IMPORTANT.—The vent cover must be kept closed at all times, except when topping-up. The electrolyte will flood if the cover is removed for long periods during or within thirty minutes of the battery being normal (6·5 amp.) charged. Single-cell discharge testers cannot be used on these batteries. Operation of the filling device will be destroyed if the battery case is drilled or punctured.

Fig. 1

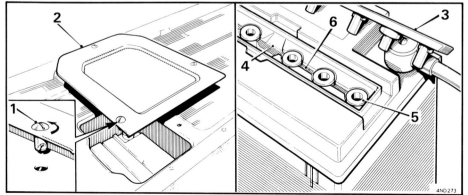

4ND273

Electrical

General maintenance The batteries must be kept dry and clean; cable and battery terminals should be smeared with petroleum jelly.

Do not leave the battery in a discharged state for any length of time. When not in regular use have the battery fully charged, and every four weeks give a short refresher trickle charge to prevent permanent damage to the battery plates.

FUSES
Fig. 2
The fuses are housed in a fuse block (1) mounted in the engine compartment body on the oil filter side of the engine.

Fuse connecting 1–2. The fuse (2) protects one parking lamp, one tail lamp, one number-plate lamp, and one front and rear side marker lamp.

Fuse connecting 3–4. The fuse (3) protects one parking lamp, one tail lamp, one number-plate lamp, and one front and rear side-marker lamp.

Fuse connecting 5–6. The fuse (4) protects the circuits which operate only when the ignition is switched on. These circuits are for the direction indicators, brake stop lamps, reverse lamps and seat belt warning. The heated back-light (when fitted) on GT models is also protected by this fuse.

Fuse connecting 7–8. The fuse (5) protects the equipment which operates independently of the ignition switch, namely horns, interior and luggage compartment lamps, headlamp flasher, brake failure warning lamp, and the cigar-lighter.

Two spare fuses (6) are provided and it is important to use the correct replacement fuse. The fusing value, current rated 17 amp. continuous (35 amp. blow rated), is marked on a coloured slip of paper inside the glass tube of the fuse.

Line fuses
Fig. 2
Running-on control valve. The 17 amp. continuous current rated (35 amp. blow rated) line fuse (7) protects the running-on control valve circuit which operates when the ignition is switched off.

Seat belt warning control unit. The 500 mA continuous current rated line fuse (8) protects the circuits within the control unit. **Under no circumstances** must any alteration be made to the specified fuse rating.

Fig. 2

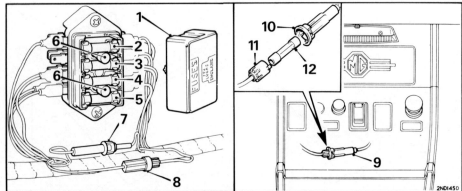

2ND145D

Hazard warning. The 17 amp. continuous current rated (35 amp. blow rated) line fuse (9) protects the hazard warning lamps and is located behind the hazard warning switch. It is accessible only when the centre console is withdrawn (see page 44).

Radio. A separate additional line fuse protects the radio (if fitted). See the instructions supplied with the radio for the correct fuse ratings.

To change a line fuse, hold one end of the cylindrical fuse holder (10), push in and twist the other end (11). Remove the fuse (12) from the cylindrical holder.

Blown fuses   A blown fuse is indicated by the failure of all the units protected by it, and is confirmed by examination of the fuse when withdrawn. Before renewing a blown fuse inspect the wiring of the units that have failed for evidence of a short-circuit or other fault.

HEADLAMPS
Light unit   To remove a light unit, ease the bottom of the outer rim (1) forwards away from
Fig. 3   the lamp. Unscrew the three inner rim retaining screws (2), remove the inner rim (3), withdraw the light unit (4), and disconnect the three-pin plug (5).

To fit a light unit, connect the three-pin plug, position the light unit in the headlamp body ensuring that the three lugs formed on the outer edge of the light unit engage in the slots formed in the body, and fit the inner retaining rim. Position the outer rim on the retaining lugs with the cut-away portion of the rim at the bottom of the lamp, press the rim downwards and inwards.

Beam setting   Two adjusting screws are provided on each headlamp for setting the main beams. The screw (6) is for adjusting the beam in the vertical plane, and the screw (7) is for horizontal adjustment. The beams must be set in accordance with local regulations; resetting and checking should be entrusted to your authorized Austin MG Dealer, who will have special equipment available for this purpose.

Fig. 3

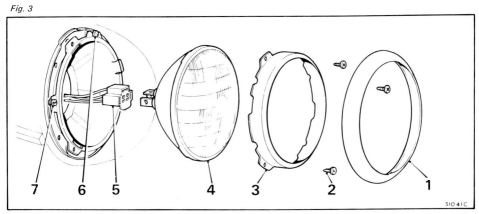

SIO 41C

Electrical

LAMPS

Parking and direction indicator
Fig. 4

To gain access to the parking and direction indicator bulb (1), unscrew the two retaining screws (2) and withdraw the rim and lens.

Stop, tail and direction indicator
Fig. 5

Remove the lens retaining screws (1) and slide the lens upwards to gain access to the direction indicator (2) and stop/tail (3) bulbs.

The direction indicator lamps have a single-filament bulb (2) which may be fitted either way round in the socket. The tail and stop lamp bulb (3) has a twin filament and offset peg bayonet fixing to ensure correct fitment.

Number-plate
Fig. 6

To change a bulb, remove the two screws (1), pull the lens (2) clear of the lamp body and unclip the bulb (3) from its contacts. When refitting, ensure that the lens engages in the seal lip and that the connectors are correctly fitted.

Side marker
Fig. 7

To renew a bulb, remove the securing screw (1) and lift off the lamp lens, noting that one end is secured by a locating tab (2). When refitting, ensure that the sealing rubber is positioned correctly and that the lens tab (2) is located beneath the lamp body rim before refitting the securing screw.

Fig. 4

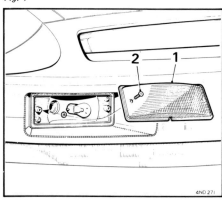

Fig. 5

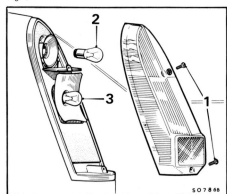

Fig. 6

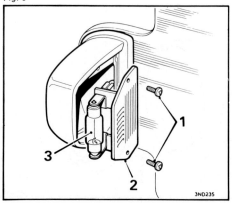

Fig. 7

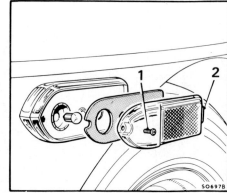

Reverse
Fig. 8
To renew a bulb, remove the two securing screws (1) and withdraw the lens. Press the bulb (2) down towards the lower contact and withdraw it from the lamp.

Fit one end of the new bulb into the hole in the lower contact, then press the top of the bulb into the lamp until the point of the cap engages the hole in the upper contact.

Luggage
Compartment
Fig. 9
The lens is held in the lamp by four locating lugs. To gain access to the bulb, gently squeeze the sides of the lens together and withdraw it from the lamp. Remove the bulb from its contacts.

Courtesy
Fig. 10
To renew a bulb, remove the two screws (1) retaining the lamp bezel and remove the bezel and lens. The bulb may then be withdrawn from its contacts.

Fig. 8

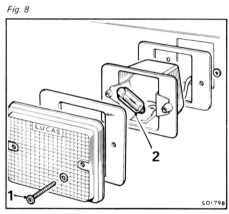

SO179B

Fig. 9

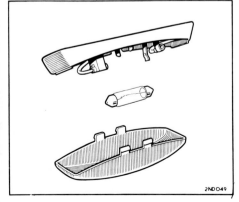

2ND049

Fig. 10

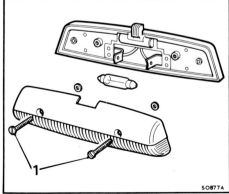

SO877A

Electrical

To gain access to the bulbs the fascia bottom panel must be removed and/or the centre console withdrawn.

Fascia bottom panel. Unscrew the three screws (1) securing the bottom panel (2) and pull the panel forward from its retaining clips (3) at the rear.

Centre console. Remove the gear-lever knob and locknut (15). Unscrew the four screws (16) securing the gaiter retaining ring, noting that the front screw is the shorter of the four screws. Raise the hinged arm-rest, unscrew the retaining screw (17) and remove the arm-rest complete with the gaiter. Unscrew the four screws (18) retaining the console and withdraw the console rearwards.

Heater control lamp bulbs. Remove the fascia bottom panel. Remove the push-fit bulb holders (4) from the controls and remove the bayonet fixing type bulb (5). To remove the air flow control illumination bulb the centre console must also be withdrawn.

Instrument panel lamp bulbs. Remove the fascia bottom panel. Remove the push-fit bulb holders (6) from the instruments and unscrew the bulbs (7).

Lights and heater booster switch bulbs. Remove the fascia bottom panel. Remove the push-fit bulb holders (8) from the switches and remove the bayonet fixing type bulbs (9). To remove the heater booster switch bulb the centre console must also be withdrawn.

Warning lamp bulbs. Remove the fascia bottom panel. Remove the push-fit bulb holders (10) from the lamps and remove the bayonet fixing type bulbs (11).

Fig. 11

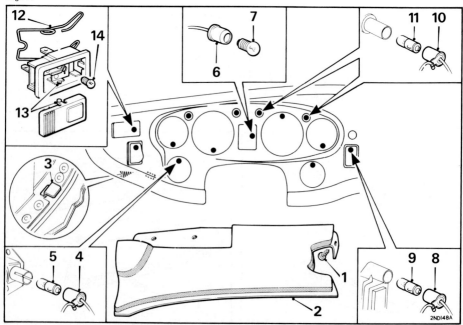

2NDI48A

Brake failure warning lamp bulb. Remove the fascia bottom panel. Remove the retaining spring clip (12) and withdraw the holder/test-push assembly from the fascia. Through the two pivot holes in the holder depress the pivot legs (13) and remove the test-push rocker from its holder. Unscrew and remove the bulb (14).

Hazard switch bulb. Withdraw the centre console. Remove the push-fit bulb holder (19) from the switch, and remove the bayonet fixing type bulb (20).

Hazard and seat belt warning lamp bulbs. Withdraw the centre console. Remove the push-fit bulb holders (21) from the lamps and remove the bayonet fixing type bulbs (22).

Cigar-lighter illumination bulb. Withdraw the centre console Squeeze the sides of the bulb hood (23) and remove the hood. Remove the bulb holder (24) from the hood clip and remove the bayonet fixing type bulb (25).

Fig. 12

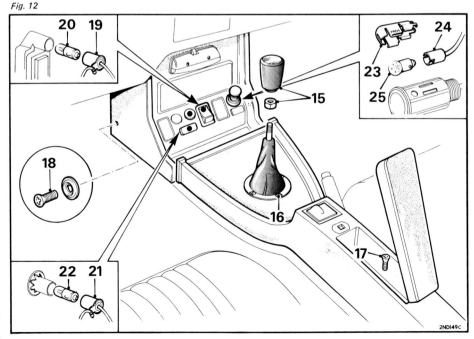

2NDI49C

		Volts	Watts	Part No.
Replacement bulbs	Headlamp (sealed beam)	12	50/40	—
	Sidelamp (with flasher)	12	5/21	GLB 380
	Stop/tail	12	5/21	GLB 380
	Reverse	12	18	BFS 273
	Number-plate lamp	12	6	GLB 254
	Direction indicator	12	21	GLB 382
	Side-marker lamp, front and rear	12	5	BFS 222
	Ignition warning	12	2	GLB 281
	Main beam	12	2	GLB 281
	Direction indicator warning lamp	12	2	GLB 281
	Brake warning lamp	12	1·5	GLB 280
	Panel illumination lamp	12	2·2	GLB 987
	Cigar-lighter illumination	12	2·2	BFS 643
	Luggage compartment lamp	12	6	GLB 254
	Courtesy lamp	12	6	GLB 254
	Hazard warning lamp	12	2	GLB 281
	Seat belt warning lamp	12	2	GLB 281
	Switch illumination	12	2	GLB 281
	Heater rotary control illumination	12	2	GLB 281

WINDSCREEN WIPER AND WASHER

Wiper arms
Fig. 13
To re-position a wiper arm on the spindle, hold the spring clip (1) clear of the retaining groove in the spindle and withdraw the arm. Replace the arm in the required position and push it down onto the spindle (2) until it is secured in position by the retaining clip.

Wiper blade
Fig. 13
To renew a wiper blade pull the arm away from the windscreen. Hold the fastener (3) and the spring retainer (4) away from the wiper arm (5) and withdraw the blade assembly from the arm.

Insert the end of the wiper arm into the spring fastener of the new blade and push the blade into engagement (6) with the arm.

To ensure efficient wiping it is recommended that wiper blades are renewed annually.

Fig. 13

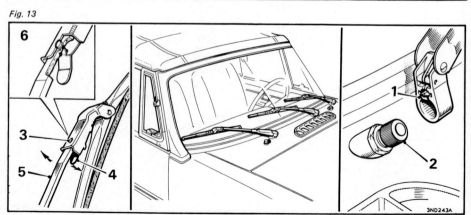

3ND243A

Windscreen washer

Fig. 14

The windscreen washer system should be checked for correct operation and the reservoir refilled if necessary every week, and before a long journey in addition to the mileage intervals given in **'MAINTENANCE SUMMARY'**.

Washer reservoir. To fill the reservoir (2), remove the cap (1).

In cold weather the washer reservoir should be filled with a mixture of water and a recommended washer solvent to prevent the water freezing.

On no account should radiator anti-freeze or methylated spirits (denatured alcohol) be used in the windscreen washer.

Jet adjusting. Turn the jet (3) using a small screwdriver to adjust the height of the spray. The spray should strike the top of the windscren.

ALTERNATOR

The following precautions must be observed to prevent inadvertent damage to the alternator and its control equipment.

Polarity. Ensure that the correct battery polarity is maintained at all times; reversed battery or charger connections will damage the alternator rectifiers.

Battery connections. The battery must never be disconnected while the engine is running.

Fig. 14

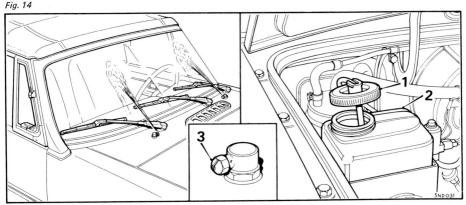

5ND031

IGNITION

Ignition timing

The ignition timing is set dynamically to give optimum engine performance with efficient engine emission control. Electronic test equipment must be used to check the ignition timing setting and the automatic advance (see **'GENERAL DATA'**). Checking and adjustment of the ignition timing setting should be carried out by your authorized Austin MG Dealer control service station.

The dynamic ignition timing must be checked after cleaning, re-setting, or renewing of the distributor contacts.

Distributor
Fig. 1

Release the retaining clips and remove the distributor cover. Remove the rotor arm (1).

Lubrication. Very lightly smear the cam (2) and pivot post (3) with grease. Add a few drops of oil to the felt pad (4) in the top of the cam spindle and through the gap (5) between the contact plate and the cam spindle to lubricate the centrifugal weights. Do **not** oil the cam wiping pad.

Every 25,000 miles in addition to the routine maintenance lubricate the contact breaker assembly centre bearing with a drop of oil in each of the two holes (6) in the base plate.

Carefully wipe away all surplus lubricant and see that the contact breaker points are perfectly clean and dry.

Cleaning distributor cover. With a nap free cloth wipe the rotor arm and the inside of the distributor cover. Refit the rotor arm and the distributor cover.

Fig. 1

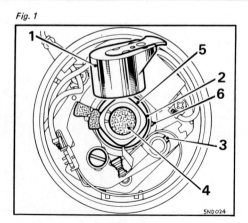

5ND024

Spark plugs
Fig. 2

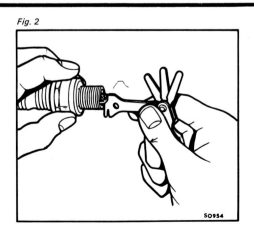

Disconnect the H.T. lead from each plug, and partly unscrew each plug. Clean the area of the cylinder head surrounding the seating of each plug, then unscrew each plug.

The spark plugs should be cleaned, preferably with an air-blast service unit.

When fitting new spark plugs ensure that only the recommended type and grade are used (see **'GENERAL DATA'**).

Check the plug gaps, and reset if necessary to the recommended gap (see **'GENERAL DATA'**). To reset, use a special Champion spark plug gauge and setting tool; move the side electrode, never the centre one.

Screw the plug down by hand as far as possible, then use a spanner for tightening only. Always use a tubular box spanner to avoid possible damage to the insulator, and do not under any circumstances use a movable wrench. Never overtighten a plug, but ensure that a good joint is made between the plug body, washer, and cylinder head. Wipe clean the outside of the plugs before reconnecting the H.T. leads.

Ignition cables   The high-tension cables connecting the distributor to the sparking plugs, may after long use, show signs of perishing. They must then be renewed using the correct type of ignition cable.

Fig. 2

SO954

ENGINE

LUBRICATION

Checking

Fig. 1

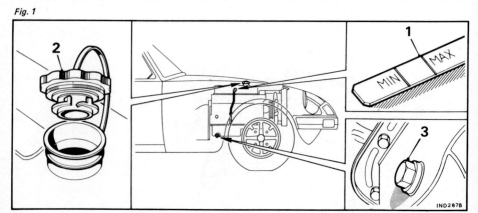

The level of the oil in the engine sump is indicated by the dipstick (1) on the right-hand side of the engine. Maintain the level between the 'MIN' and 'MAX' mark on the dipstick and never allow it to fall below the 'MIN' mark.

The filler (2) is on the forward end of the rocker cover and is provided with a quick-action cap.

Ensure that the dipstick is correctly refitted.

The oil level should always be checked before a long journey.

Draining

To drain the engine oil, remove the drain plug (3) located on the right-hand side at the rear of the sump. This operation should be carried out while the engine is warm.

Clean the drain plug; check that its copper sealing washer is in a satisfactory condition, and refit.

Filling

Fill the engine with the correct quantity (see **'GENERAL DATA'**) of a recommended oil. Run the engine for a short while then allow it to stand for a few minutes before checking the level with the dipstick.

Fig. 1

IND287B

Emission
Control System
Warranty
for 1975 models

British Leyland Motors Inc.
600 Willow Tree Road, Leonia, New Jersey 07605

Warranty Applicable to the Emission Control System

British Leyland Motors Inc., 600 Willow Tree Road, Leonia, New Jersey 07605, warrants to the ultimate purchaser and each subsequent purchaser of the vehicle that it has been designed, built and equipped so as to conform at the time of sale with all U.S. emission standards applicable at the time of manufacture, and that it is free from defects in materials and workmanship which would cause it not to meet these standards for five years from the first retail delivery of the vehicle or 50,000 miles, whichever occurs first. Failures which result from lack of proper maintenance or from misuse or abuse of the vehicle or engine are not covered by this Warranty.

Like any other piece of complicated machinery, the car will need regular attention and service to make sure that the Emission Control Systems continue to function properly. This is the owner's responsibility. The manufacturer cannot guarantee that emissions will not rise to unacceptable levels if maintenance of the Systems is not carefully and regularly carried out.

The Warranty guarantees the Emission Control Systems to be free of 'defects'. Ordinary wear and tear on the vehicle and the engine, sufficient to require replacement of parts and components at regular Maintenance Intervals as specified in the Handbook, is not evidence of a 'defect'. For example, spark plugs, catalytic converter and muffler will require replacement; engine valves, an important component of the Emission Control System, should be checked and adjusted where necessary as specified in the instructions. Full details are in the Handbook or Manual. The manufacturer cannot accept responsibility for any condition claimed to be a 'defect' if it results from a failure to follow the manufacturer's service instructions.

Failure of the Emission Control Systems may also result from misuse or abuse. Operation of the car at excessive speeds, or overloaded, or under heavy dust condition, may adversely affect the functioning of the Emission Control Systems, as may racing the car, or fire or accident caused to the car. If the car is operated only on short trips, or is not, generally speaking, driven each day for at least several miles, some components of the Emission Control Systems may deteriorate more rapidly than would otherwise be expected, and this does not show a 'defect'.

When replacement parts are used, it is essential that they be of proper design and performance specifications. For example, use of the wrong spark plugs may seriously prejudice emission levels. British Leyland Dealers are fully trained and equipped to use proper parts, either manufactured by or approved by British Leyland. Any failure resulting from the use of non-approved replacement parts will not be considered a 'defect', and the warranty will be void.

The 'Passport to Service' contains blanks to be filled in as maintenance of the systems is done at recommended intervals. It is extremely important that this record be kept up to date so that it may be consulted if any question arises about the continued validity of the Emission Control Warranty.

If replacement of any component at the manufacturer's cost is necessary under the Emission Control Warranty, the work (including parts and labour) should be performed by an authorized British Leyland Dealer, unless written approval has first been secured from British Leyland for use of another service facility.

Regular maintenance of the systems may be done by an authorized British Leyland Dealer or by other established and qualified service facilities. Authorized dealers will, of course, be fully equipped and trained to keep the systems in proper running order, and will have approved spare parts that can be used. If service work is done by other service facilities, it is recommended that copies of the repair orders be kept to show that the services were properly performed and approved replacement parts were used.

Because of local legal requirements, or because of engine characteristics, some cars are equipped with Catalytic converters as part of the Emission Control Systems. Catalytic converters are used to reduce carbon monoxide and hydrocarbon emissions through the exhaust system.

If you see a label reading **'UNLEADED GASOLINE ONLY'** or **'UNLEADED FUEL ONLY'** on your fuel gauge or near it on the dashboard, you have a Catalytic converter equipped car. Damage caused by the use of leaded fuel or by driving the vehicle with a persistent misfiring of the engine will not be covered by this Warranty.

Oil filter changing
Fig. 2

The oil filter is a disposable cartridge type.

To renew, unscrew the cartridge (1) from the filter head (2) and discard the cartridge.

NOTE.—If difficulty in unscrewing the cartridge is experienced, consult your authorized Austin MG Dealer.

Smear the new seal (3) with engine oil and fit it into its groove in the new cartridge. Screw the cartridge to the filter head using hand force only.

Refill the engine with the correct quantity of a recommended lubricant, start the engine and check for oil leakage.

DRIVE BELT

Alternator
Fig. 3

Tension. When correctly tensioned, a total deflection of $\frac{1}{2}$ in. under moderate hand pressure, should be possible at the midway point of the longest belt run between the pulleys.

Adjusting. To adjust the belt tension, slacken the securing bolts (1) and adjusting link nuts (2), and move the alternator to the required position. Apply any leverage necessary to the alternator end bracket (3) only and not to any other part; to avoid damaging the drive-end bracket the lever should preferably be of wood or soft metal. Tighten the bolts and re-check the belt tension. **DO NOT OVERTIGHTEN** as this will impose an excess loading on the drive bearings.

Fig. 2

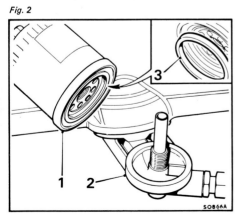

S0866A

Fig. 3

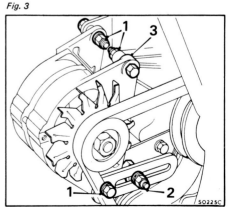

S0225C

Engine

VALVE ROCKER CLEARANCE

Checking
Fig. 4

Disconnect the purge line (1) from the rocker cover. Remove the rocker cover (2) and insert a 0·013 in. feeler gauge (3) between the valve rocker arms and the valve stem. The gauge should be a sliding fit when the engine is warm. Check each clearance in the following order:

Check No. 1 valve with No. 8 fully open. Check No. 8 valve with No. 1 fully open.

,,	,, 3 ,,	,, ,, 6 ,,	,,	,, ,, 6 ,,	,, ,, 3 ,,	,,
,,	,, 5 ,,	,, ,, 4 ,,	,,	,, ,, 4 ,,	,, ,, 5 ,,	,,
,,	,, 2 ,,	,, ,, 7 ,,	,,	,, ,, 7 ,,	,, ,, 2 ,,	,,

Adjusting
Fig. 4

Slacken the adjusting screw locknut on the opposite end of the rocker arm and rotate the screw clockwise to reduce the clearance or anti-clockwise to increase it. Retighten the locknut when the clearance is correct, holding the screw against rotation with a screwdriver.

Cleaning
Fig. 4

Clean the rocker cover sealing face. Examine the orifice (4) of the restrictor for obstruction. Clean any dirt or deposit from the restrictor orifice, using a length of soft wire.

Refitting
Fig. 4

Check the rocker cover gasket (5) for damage. Fit a new gasket if necessary. Refit the cover and connect the purge line. Check that the oil filler cap (6) seals correctly; renew it if necessary.

Fig. 4

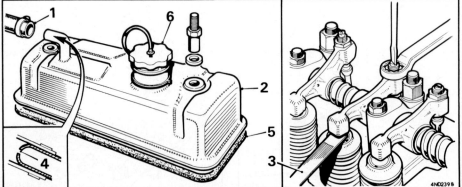

EMISSION CONTROL SYSTEMS

You and each subsequent owner of the car are urged to make sure that the recommended maintenance procedures are carried out at the intervals specified. For the emission controls to continue to function effectively, it is strongly recommended that you arrange for regular maintenance inspections to be carried out by your authorized Austin MG Dealer or by any other qualified service outlet which regularly performs such service on British Leyland cars.

You have been provided with a Passport to Service which contains a facility to record that maintenance has been carried out at the recommended mileages.

You should have the maintenance record completed by your authorized Austin MG Dealer (or by other dealer or station equipped to render such service) at the regular mileage intervals indicated in the Maintenance Summary. The Handbook and Passport to Service should be handed to subsequent purchasers of the vehicle at the time of sale so that the maintenance instructions are available and that the record of maintenance can be continued.

You are also urged to study with care the section covering 'MALFUNCTION IDENTIFICATION'. Study of this section will be of aid to you in detecting possible malfunctions of the emission controls so that necessary service measures can immediately be taken.

IMPORTANT

Your attention is particularly drawn to the following:

1. Maintenance and service charges applicable to the emission control system are not covered by the warranty and are not reimbursable, unless shown to have been caused by defects in materials and workmanship covered by the warranty.

2. The engine has not been designed for the regular use of unleaded or low lead gasoline and the use of such fuels cannot be recommended as they could have a detrimental effect on engine components, resulting in loss of performance, excess exhaust emissions and possibly complete engine failure.

General description This section gives a general description of the crankcase, exhaust and fuel evaporative emission control systems fitted to this vehicle and the function of their individual components. It must be emphasized that correct carburetter adjustment and ignition timing which have been pre-set at the factory are essential for the efficient functioning of the exhaust emission controls. Should it become necessary to check these settings this work should be carried out by an authorized Austin MG or British Leyland Dealer who has the specialist equipment and training to undertake these adjustments.

The basic engine tuning data will be found on the emission control information label located in the front of the engine compartment.

Emission Control Systems

Crankcase emission control The engine crankcase breather outlet incorporates an oil separator flame-trap which is connected by hoses to the controlled depression chamber between the piston and the throttle disc valve of the carburetter. Piston blowby fumes are drawn into the depression chamber where they combine with the engine inlet charge for combustion in the engine cylinders in the normal way. Fresh filtered air is supplied to the engine crankcase through a hose connected between the engine valve rocker cover and the charcoal canister of the fuel evaporative emission control system.

THE EMISSION CONTROL COMPONENTS

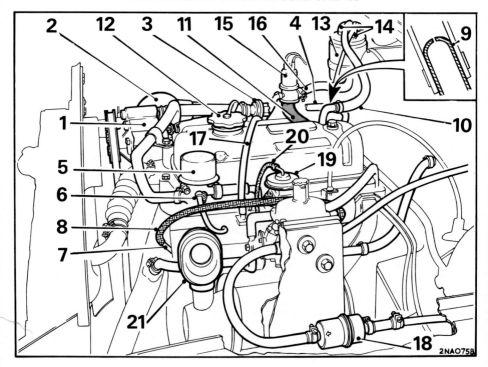

1. Air pump	12. Sealed oil filler cap
2. Air pump air cleaner	13. Charcoal adsorption canister
3. Check valve	14. Vapour lines
4. Air manifold	15. Running-on control valve
5. Gulp valve	16. Running-on control hose
6. Sensing pipe	17. Running-on control pipe
7. Oil separator/flame trap	18. Fuel line filter
8. Breather pipe	19. Exhaust gas recirculation (E.G.R.) valve
9. Restricted connection	20. E.G.R. valve hose
10. Purge line	21. Air temperature control valve
11. Air vent pipe	

Exhaust emission control

The exhaust emission control system is designed to give the required degree of control of the carbon monoxide, unburnt hydrocarbons and oxides of nitrogen content of exhaust gases.

The exhaust emission control system is a combination of engine components and air injection techniques and consists of a special carburetter, air injection into the exhaust ports and exhaust gas recirculation.

The quantity of air-polluting elements in the gases leaving the exhaust pipe is reduced by adding air to the hot gases immediately they leave the combustion chambers of the engine. The injection of air into the exhaust gases promotes a continued conversion of the undesirable hydrocarbon and carbon monoxide components of the exhaust gases to relatively harmless carbon dioxide and water.

The exhaust gas recirculation valve mounted on the exhaust manifold will re-circulate a controlled quantity of the exhaust gases to reduce combustion chamber temperature.

An air pump mounted on the front of the engine, and belt-driven from the water pump pulley, supplies air under pressure through hoses and a check valve and distribution manifold to injectors in each exhaust port in the engine cylinder head. The check valve prevents high pressure exhaust gases from blowing back into the air pump due to, for example, pump drive failure.

Air from the pump is also supplied to a gulp valve, the outlet of which is connected to the engine inlet manifold. A small-bore sensing pipe connected between the inlet manifold and the diaphragm chamber of the gulp valve relays changes in manifold depression to the valve which will open under certain conditions such as those created by deceleration or engine overrun.

When the gulp valve opens, a small quantity of air is admitted directly into the inlet manifold to lean off the rich air/fuel mixture which is present in the manifold under conditions immediately following throttle closure. This mixture, having been reduced to a burnable condition, combines with engine inlet charge for combustion in the engine cylinders in the normal way.

The carburetter is manufactured to a special exhaust emission specification and is tuned to give the maximum emission control consistent with retaining vehicle performance and drivability. The metering needle is arranged in such a manner that it is always lightly spring loaded against the side of the jet to ensure consistency of fuel metering. A throttle by-pass valve limits the inlet manifold depression and ensures that during conditions of engine overrun the air/fuel mixture enters the engine cylinders in a burnable condition consistent with low emission levels.

Emission Control Systems

Fuel evaporative loss control To prevent air pollution by vapours from the fuel tank and carburetter vents, the control equipment stores the vapour in a charcoal-filled canister while the engine is stopped and disposes of it via the engine crankcase emission control system when the engine is running.

The fuel tank venting is designed to ensure that no liquid fuel is carried to the storage canister with the vapours and that vapours are vented through the control system.

The capacity of the fuel tank is limited by a specially positioned filler vent tube and ensures sufficient volume is available after filling to accommodate fuel which would otherwise be displaced as a result of a high temperature rise.

Warning: When filling with fuel do not attempt to add more than the capacity given in **'GENERAL DATA'.** Slow filling, or allowing the level to drop and then adding more fuel, is not recommended and **can result in spillage due to expansion.**

THE LAYOUT OF THE FUEL EVAPORATIVE LOSS CONTROL SYSTEM

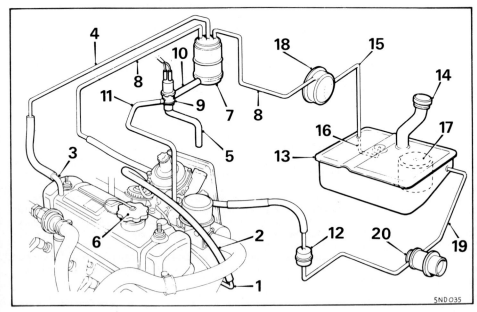

5ND035

1. Oil separator/flame trap	11. Running-on control pipe
2. Breather pipe	12. Fuel line filter
3. Restrictor connection	13. Fuel tank
4. Purge line	14. Sealed fuel filler cap
5. Air vent pipe	15. Vapour line
6. Sealed oil filler cap	16. Vapour tube
7. Charcoal adsorption canister	17. Capacity limiting tank
8. Vapour lines	18. Separation tank
9. Running-on control valve	19. Fuel pipe
10. Running-on control hose	20. Fuel pump

MALFUNCTION IDENTIFICATION

Check the following items regularly for visual signs of a malfunction and also if any of the Driving Symptoms listed should persistently occur. **If you are unable to locate and/or correct the malfunction you are advised to contact your authorized Austin MG Dealer immediately.**

Visual checks
1. Condition and adjustment of drive belts.
2. Baked or overheated hose between air pump and check valve.
3. All hoses for security, damage and deterioration.
4. Fuel leakage.
5. Oil filler cap for sealing.
6. E.G.R. warning light on.

Driving symptoms
1. Violent backfire in exhaust system.
2. Hesitation to accelerate on re-opening the throttle after sudden throttle closure.
3. Engine idles erratically or stalls.
4. Noisy air pump.
5. Ignition warning light on above idle speed (slack or broken fan belt).
6. Smell of fuel vapours.
7. Engine stops after short running periods (fuel starvation).
8. Lack of power.
9. High fuel consumption.
10. Engine misfire.
11. High temperature indicated (overheating of coolant).

Emission Control Systems

MAINTENANCE OPERATIONS

All items marked † in the 'MAINTENANCE SUMMARY' given on pages 70 to 76 are emission control related.

Adsorption canister
Fig. 1

The charcoal adsorption canister (5) must be renewed every 25,000 miles.

To remove the canister. Unscrew the windscreen washer reservoir cap (1), withdraw the tube from the reservoir and remove the reservoir (2) from its mounting. Disconnect the air vent pipe (3), vapour lines (4) and purge pipe (5) from their connections on the canister. Remove the securing bracket, nut and bolt (6), collecting the spacer, and remove the canister (7).

Refitting. When refitting, ensure that all connections to the canister are secure. Locate the windscreen washer reservoir on its mounting, insert the tube and fit the cap.

To prevent the engine running on after the ignition has been switched off a control valve is fitted to the air vent pipe of the adsorption canister. The valve is a self-contained unit and requires no regular maintenance. Care should be taken when renewing the adsorption canister not to disturb the valve or its connections.

Fuel line filter
Fig. 2

The filter assembly must be renewed every 12,500 miles.

Removing. Remove the screw (1) to release the carburetter feed hose retaining clip. Slacken the clip and remove the carburetter feed hose (2) from the filter. Slacken the clip and remove the fuel tank delivery hose (3) from the filter. Remove and discard the filter (4). When refitting a new filter ensure that the flow arrow is directed towards the carburetter feed hose.

Purge line restrictor

To check, disconnect the purge line from the rocker cover elbow. Examine the orifice of the restriction formed in the elbow for obstruction. Clear any dirt or deposits from the restrictor orifice, using a length of wire, see page 52.

Fig. 1

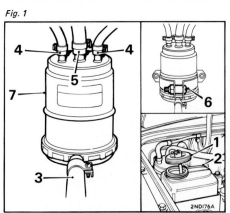

2NDI76A

Fig. 2

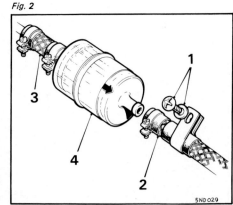

5ND029

Air pump

The element of the air pump air cleaner must be renewed every 12,500 miles or 12 months; more frequent changes may be necessary in dusty operating conditions.

Air cleaner element changing (Fig. 3). Remove the nut and washer (1). Withdraw the cover (2) and discard the element (3). Clean the inside of the cover thoroughly and reassemble using a new element.

Drive belt tension. When correctly tensioned, a total deflection of $\frac{1}{2}$ in. under moderate hand pressure, should be possible at the midway point of the belt run.

Adjusting (Fig. 4). Slacken the securing bolt (1) and the two adjusting link bolts (2), move the air pump to the required position. Tighten the bolts and re-check the belt tension. **DO NOT OVERTIGHTEN.**

Fig. 3

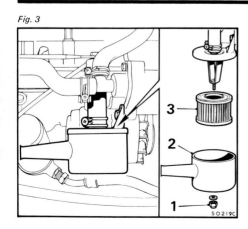

Fig. 4

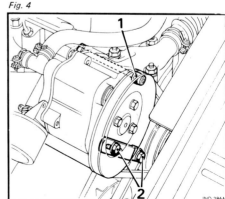

Emission Control Systems

Filler caps
Fig. 5

Both the engine oil filler cap (1) and the fuel tank filler cap (2) are non-venting and form a seal on the filling apertures.

IT IS ESSENTIAL TO THE SATISFACTORY OPERATION OF THE EVAPORATIVE LOSS SYSTEM THAT BOTH CAPS ARE ALWAYS REFITTED CORRECTLY AND TIGHTENED FULLY. A DEFECTIVE CAP OR CAP SEAL (3) MUST BE REPLACED.

Exhaust gas recirculation valve
Fig. 6

The E.G.R. valve warning light (1) will glow when the car has completed a distance of 25,000 miles, indicating to the driver that the valve (2) should be serviced. At the same time the service interval counter will show the mileage percentage that has elapsed in a 25,000 mile period.

Servicing the E.G.R. valve should be carried out by your authorized Austin MG Dealer who on completion will reset the service interval counter to zero, and cancel the warning light illumination.

Fig. 5

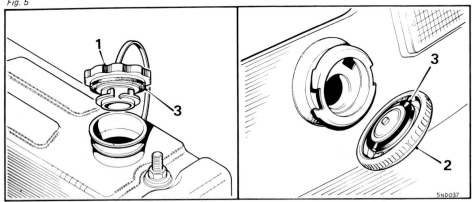

Fig. 6

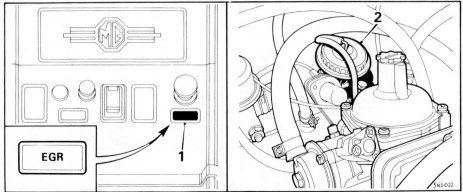

FUEL SYSTEM

AIR CLEANER

The element of the air cleaner must be renewed every 12,500 miles; more frequent changes may be necessary in dusty operating conditions.

Element changing
Fig. 1

Unscrew the wing nut (1), pivot the end cover away from the engine to release the air temperature control valve from the hot air hose (2), and remove the end cover (3) and end cap (4). Withdraw the element (5) and discard it.

Thoroughly clean the air cleaner cover, cap and the casing (6). Fit a new element. Refit the end cap, ensuring that its lip (7) supports the inside of the filter element. Locate the end cover in position, connect the air temperature control valve to the hot air hose, fit and tighten the wing nut.

Air intake temperature control
Fig. 1

The temperature of the air entering the carburetter is controlled by a valve fitted to the intake of the air cleaner. The control valve (8) should be inspected for condition and operation by your authorized Austin MG Dealer.

Fig. 1

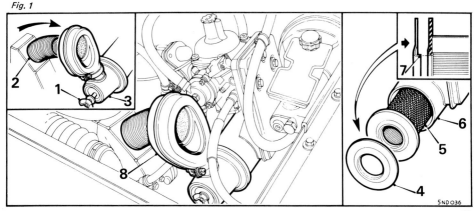

5ND036

Fuel System

CARBURETTER

Air pollution control

The carburetter incorporates features which assist in reducing exhaust emissions. Maladjustment or the fitting of parts not to the required specification may render these features ineffective.

Carburetter damper
Fig. 2

Checking oil level. Unscrew the damper cap (4) from the carburetter top cover. Carefully raise the damper to the top of its travel. Lower the damper back into the hollow piston rod. If the oil level in the hollow piston rod is correct, resistance should be felt when there is a gap of approximately $\frac{1}{4}$ in. (A) between the cap and the carburetter top cover. Top up if necessary. Screw the damper cap firmly in the carburetter top cover.

Topping up the oil level. Detach the throttle cam return springs (1) from the air cleaner. Remove the three bolts (2) securing the air cleaner to the carburetter, noting that the top bolt secures the brake servo vacuum hose clip. Detach the air temperature control valve from the hot air hose (3) and manœuvre the air cleaner forwards in the engine compartment.

Unscrew the damper cap (4) from the carburetter top cover. Raise the piston (5) with a finger, and at the same time lift the damper (4) and carefully ease the retaining cap (6) from the hollow piston rod to release the damper assembly from the piston. With the piston raised, top up the hollow piston rod with a recommended engine oil until the level is $\frac{1}{4}$ in. below the top of the hollow piston rod. Lower the piston. **UNDER NO CIRCUMSTANCES SHOULD A HEAVY BODIED LUBRICANT BE USED.** Ensure the oil level is correct. Raise the piston and carefully press the retaining cup into the hollow piston rod. Screw the damper cap firmly into the carburetter top cover.

Check the condition of the air cleaner gasket, renew if necessary. Connect the air temperature control valve to the hot air hose and secure the air cleaner to the carburetter.

Tuning

The tuning of the carburetter is confined to setting the idle speed and mixture strength (CO percentage). Adjustment should only be undertaken by your authorized Austin MG Dealer who will have the essential special equipment for this purpose.

Fig. 2

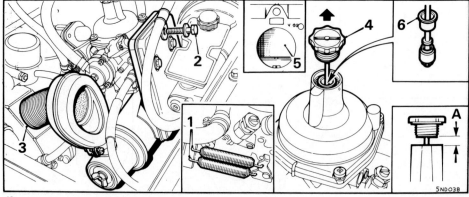

TRANSMISSION

GEARBOX   *Fig. 1*

Checking   From underneath the car, remove the fuel level filler plug (1) and check the oil level. The correct level is at bottom of the filler level plug hole.

OVERDRIVE   *Fig. 1*

Draining   Remove the plug (2) to drain the oil from the gearbox and overdrive unit.

Sump filter   Drain the gearbox and overdrive unit.

Clean the sump cover and its surroundings. Remove the cover securing screws, withdraw the cover (3) and the filter (4). Clean all metallic particles from the two magnets fitted to the inside of the cover, wash the cover and filter in gasoline. Refit the filter and cover.

Relief valve filter   Remove the plug and the seal (5); withdraw the relief valve approximately $\frac{1}{2}$ in. and remove the filter (6). Wash the filter, plug and seal in gasoline.

Fit the filter to the relief valve, push the valve fully home and refit the plug and seal.

Filling   Fill the gearbox and overdrive unit through the combined oil filler (1) with the correct quantity (see **'GENERAL DATA'**) of one of the recommended oils. Run the car for a short distance, allow it to stand for a few minutes, then re-check the level with the dipstick. **Anti-friction additives must not be used in the gearbox or overdrive.**

Fig. 1

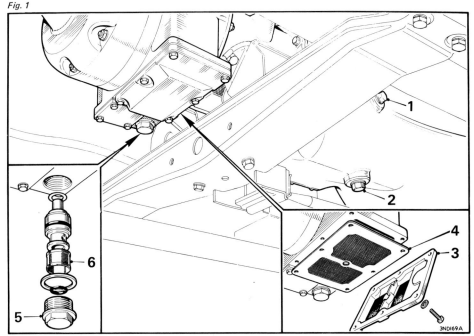

3ND169A

Transmission

REAR AXLE
Checking
Fig. 2

A combined oil filler and level plug (1) is located on the rear of the axle. The oil level must be maintained at the bottom of the plug aperture; ensure that the car is standing level when checking. After topping up the oil level, allow sufficient time for any surplus oil which may have been added to run out of the aperture before replacing the plug.

Do not drain the rear axle when the After-sales Service is carried out.

PROPELLER SHAFT
Lubrication
Fig. 3

A nipple (1) is provided at the front end of the propeller shaft for lubricating the sliding yoke. To lubricate, give three or four strokes of a gun filled with a recommended grease.

Fig. 2

Fig. 3

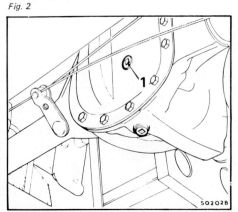

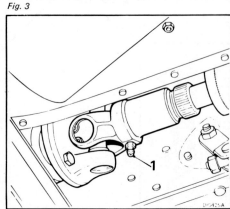

STEERING/SUSPENSION

Wheel alignment
Fig. 1

Incorrect wheel alignment can cause excessive and uneven tyre wear. The front wheels must be set so that the distance 'A' is $\frac{1}{16}$ in. to $\frac{3}{32}$ in. (toe in) less than the distance 'B'.

Wheel alignment requires the use of a special gauge and this work should be entrusted to your authorized Austin MG Dealer.

Lubrication
Fig. 2

The three lubricating nipples (arrowed) on each of the swivel pins should be charged periodically with one of the recommended greases.

Steering rack

Inspect the gaiters or bellows of the steering rack for leakage of lubricant and deterioration. If leakage of lubricant is evident, consult your authorized Austin MG Dealer.

Fig. 1

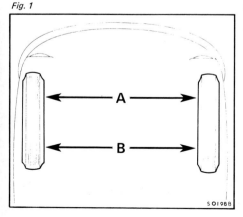

Fig. 2

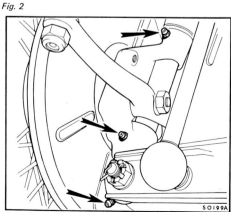

During running-in from new certain adjustments vary from the specification figures detailed. They will be set to specification by your authorized Austin MG Dealer at the **After-Sales Service** and should thereafter be maintained throughout the car's life.

Engine

Type	18V 797AE Standard	
	18V 798AE Overdrive	
Bore	3·16 in	80·26 mm
Stroke	3·5 in	89 mm
No. of cylinders	4	
Capacity	110 in³	1800 cc
Compression ratio	8 : 1	
Firing order	1, 3, 4, 2	
Valve clearance cold	0·013 in	0·33 mm
Oil pressure: Idling	10 to 25 lbf/in²	0·17 to 1·7 kgf/cm²
Normal	50 to 80 lbf/in²	3·5 to 5·6 kgf/cm²
Idle speed	850 rev/min	
Exhaust gas content analyser reading at idle speed	5½ ± 1% CO maximum	

Ignition

Stroboscopic ignition timing ..	13° B.T.D.C. at 1500 rev/min
Timing marks	Notch on crankshaft pulley, pointers on timing chain cover
Contact breaker gap	0·014 to 0·016 in 0·36 to 0·41 mm
Sparking plugs	Champion N-9Y
Plug gap	0·035 in 0·90 mm

Fuel system

Recommended octane rating ..	See page 26
Carburetter	Zenith Stromberg type 175 CD5T
Fuel pump	S.U. type AUF 300 electric

Gearbox and overdrive

Overdrive ratio	0·82 : 1		
Overall ratios: First	11·867 : 1		
Second	8·47 : 1		*Overdrive*
Third	5·40 : 1		4·43 : 1
Fourth	3·909 : 1		3·20 : 1
Reverse	12·098 : 1		

Top gear speed per 1,000 rev/min:

Standard	18 m.p.h. (29 km/h)
Overdrive	22 m.p.h. (35 km/h)

Capacities	Fuel tank	12 U.S. gal	10 gal	45·4 litres
	Cooling system	11·4 U.S. pt	9½ pt	5·4 litres
	Cooling system with heater..	12 U.S. pt	10 pt	5·6 litres
	Engine sump	6 U.S. pt	5¼ pt	3 litres
	Engine sump with filter change ..	7·25 U.S. pt	6 pt	3·4 litres
	Gearbox	6 U.S. pt	5 pt	2·84 litres
	Gearbox with overdrive ..	7·25 U.S. pt	6 pt	3·4 litres
	Rear axle	2 U.S. pt	1½ pt	0·85 litre

Dimensions	Length	13 ft 2¼ in	4 m
	Width	4 ft 11$\frac{15}{16}$ in	152·3 cm
	Height, hood erected ..	4 ft 2⅞ in	129·2 cm
	Ground clearance (minimum) ..	4$\frac{3}{16}$ in	106 mm
	Track: Front	4 ft 1 in	124·4 cm
	Rear	4 ft 1¼ in	125 cm
	Wheelbase	7 ft 7⅛ in	231·5 cm
	Turning circle '	32 ft	9·75 m
	Toe in	$\frac{1}{16}$ to $\frac{3}{32}$ in	1·5 to 2·3 mm

Wheels and tyres	Wheel size: Pressed spoked ..	5J FH × 14	
	Wire	4½J × 14 (60-spoke)	
	Tyres:	Size	Type
	Tourer	165SR—14	Radial-ply

Tyre pressures

Condition	Front			Rear		
	lbf/in²	kgf/cm²	bars	lbf/in²	kgf/cm²	bars
Normal car weight	21	1·48	1·45	24	1·69	1·66
Gross car weight and sustained speed	21	1·48	1·45	26	1·83	1·79

It is recommended that for sustained speeds at near maximum the above tyre pressures are increased by 6 lbf/in² (0·42 kgf/cm², 0·32 bars).

Refer to page 68 for 'Weights'

General Data

Weights

Loading conditions		Total weight	Distribution	
			Front	*Rear*
Kerbside	Including full fuel tank and all optional extras	2290 lb (1039 kg)	1157 lb (525 kg)	1133 lb (514 kg)
Normal	Kerbside weight including driver and passenger	2590 lb (1174 kg)	1266 lb (574 kg)	1324 lb (600 kg)
Gross	Maximum weight condition, refer to note below	2710 lb (1229 kg)	1242 lb (563 kg)	1468 lb (666 kg)
Maximum permissible towing weight		1680 lb (762 kg)		
Recommended towbar hitch load		100 lb (45 kg)		

NOTE: Due consideration must be given to the overall weight when fully loading the car. Any loads carried on a luggage rack or downward load from a towing hitch must also be included in the maximum loading.

SERVICE

Service parts and accessories Genuine BRITISH LEYLAND and UNIPART parts and accessories are designed and tested for your vehicle and have the full backing of the British Leyland Factory Warranty.

Genuine British Leyland and UNIPART parts and accessories are supplied in cartons and packs bearing either or both of these symbols.

Identification When communicating with your Distributor or Dealer always quote the commission and engine numbers. When the communication concerns the transmission units or body details it is necessary to quote also the transmission casing and body numbers.

Body number. Stamped on a plate secured to the left-hand side of the bonnet lock platform.

Car number. Stamped on a plate secured to left-hand door post.

Engine number. Stamped on a plate secured to the right-hand side of the cylinder block.

Gearbox number. Stamped on the left-hand side of the gearbox casing.

Rear axle number. Stamped on the front of the left-hand rear axle tube near the spring seating.

Supplementary tool kit A Tool Kit is obtainable from all authorized Austin MG Dealers. The kit, in a waterproof roll, contains the following tools:

8 combination spanners	3 screwdrivers
1 adjustable spanner	1 feeler gauge set
2 pairs pliers	

British Leyland Motors Inc.

600 Willow Tree Road, Leonia
New Jersey 07605
Telephone: (201) 461/7300   *Telex.* 135491

British Leyland Motors Canada Limited

4445 Fairview Street
P.O. Box 5033
Burlington · Ontario · Canada
Telephone: (416) 632/3040   *Telex:* 021678

MAINTENANCE SUMMARY

Basic engine tuning data will be found on the Vehicle Emission Control Information label located in the engine compartment.

Detailed maintenance instructions will be found on the page indicated after each item.

The following items should be checked weekly by the driver:
Engine oil level (50)
Brake fluid level (37)
Radiator coolant level (30)
Battery electrolyte level (39)
Windshield washer reservoir fluid level (47)
All tyre pressures (34)
All lights for operation
Horn operation
Windshield wipers operation

MAINTENANCE INTERVALS

† These items are emission related

Service	Mileage × 1000	Monthly intervals	Page No.
A	1	After Sales Service	70
B	3, 9, 16, 22, 28, 34, 41, 47	3	71
C	6, 19, 31, 44	6	72
D	12·5, 37·5	12	73
E	25, 50	24	75

NOTE: The service intervals are based on an annual mileage of approximately 12,500 miles. Should the vehicle complete substantially less miles than this per annum, it is recommended that a 'C' service is completed at six-month intervals, and a 'D' service at twelve-month intervals.

'A' SERVICE

Lubrication
Lubricate all grease points (excluding hubs).
Renew engine oil (50).
Check/top up brake fluid reservoir (37).
Check/top up clutch fluid reservoir (36)
Check/top up battery electrolyte (39).
Check top up cooling system (30).
Check/top up rear axle (64).
Drain gearbox, refill with new oil (non overdrive) (63).
Drain gearbox and overdrive, clean filters and refill with new oil (63)
Check/top up screen washer reservoir (47).
†Lubricate distributor (48).
†Lubricate accelerator control linkage and pedal pivot; check operation (78).
Lubricate all locks and hinges (not steering lock).

Engine
†Check driving belts; adjust or renew (51 and 59).
Check cooling system hoses/pipes for security and condition.
†Check crankcase breathing and evaporative loss system. Check hoses/pipes for security.
†Check air injection system hoses/pipes for security.
†Check security of engine bolts and mountings.
†Check/adjust torque of cylinder head nuts.
†Check/adjust valve clearance (52).
†Check security of E.G.R. valve operating lines.
†Check exhaust system for leaks and security.

70

Ignition
†Check ignition wiring for fraying, chafing and deterioration.
†Check/adjust dwell angle and ignition timing, using electronic equipment.

Fuel system
†Check fuel system for leaks.
†Top up carburetter piston damper (62).
†Check/adjust carburetter idle settings.

Safety
Check tyres for tread depth, visually for cuts in tyre fabric, exposure of ply and cord structure, lumps and bulges.
Check/adjust tyre pressures, including spare (34).
Check tightness of road wheel fastenings (32).
Check condition and security of steering unit, joints and gaiters.
Check security of suspension fixings.
Check steering and suspension for oil/fluid leaks.
Check brake servo hoses/pipes for security.
Check/adjust foot and hand brake (35).
Check visually hydraulic pipes and unions for chafing, leaks and corrosion.
Check/adjust front wheel alignment.
Check output of charging system.
Check function of original equipment, i.e. interior and exterior lamps, horns, warning indicators, windscreen wipers and washers.
Check/adjust headlamp alignment.
Check instrumentation.
Check operation of all door locks and window controls.

Road test
Road/roller test and check operation of all instrumentation.
Report additional work required.

'B' SERVICE

Lubrication
Lubricate all grease points (excluding hubs) (78).
Check/top up engine oil (50).
Check/top up brake fluid reservoir (37).
Check/top up clutch fluid reservoir (36)
Check/top up battery electrolyte (39).
Check/top up cooling system (30).
Check/top up gearbox and rear axle oils (63 and 64).
Check/top up screen washer reservoir (47).

Engine
†Check fan drive belt; adjust or renew (51).
†Check exhaust system for leaks and security.

Maintenance Summary

‘B’ SERVICE—*continued*

Fuel system
†Check fuel system for leaks.

Safety
   Check tyres for tread depth, visually for cuts in tyre fabric, exposure of ply or cord structure, lumps or bulges.
   Check that tyres comply with manufacturer's specification (67).
   Check/adjust tyre pressures, including spare (34).
   Check tightness of road wheel fastenings (32).
   Check condition and security of steering unit, joints and gaiters.
   Check steering and suspension for oil/fluid leaks.
   Check/adjust foot and hand brake (35).
   Check visually hydraulic pipes and unions for chafing, leaks and corrosion.
   Check function of original equipment, i.e. interior and exterior lamps, horns, warning indicators, windscreen wipers and washers.
   Check, if necessary renew, wiper blades (46).
   Check/adjust headlamp alignment.

‘C’ SERVICE

Lubrication
   Lubricate all grease points (excluding hubs) (78).
   Renew engine oil and filter (50).
   Check/top up brake fluid reservoir (37).
   Check/top up clutch fluid reservoir (36).
   Check/top up battery electrolyte (39).
   Check/top up cooling system (30).
   Check/top up gearbox and rear axle oils (63 and 64).
   Check/top up screen washer reservoir (47).
†Lubricate distributor (48).
†Lubricate accelerator control linkage and pedal pivot; check operation (78).
   Lubricate all locks and hinges (not steering lock).

Engine
†Check fan drive belt; adjust or renew (51).
   Check cooling system hoses/pipes for security and condition.
†Check exhaust system for leaks and security.

Ignition
†Clean spark plugs (49).

Fuel system
†Check fuel system for leaks.

72

'C' SERVICE—*continued*
Safety
Check tyres for tread depth, visually for cuts in tyre fabric, exposure of ply or cord structure, lumps and bulges.
Check that tyres comply with manufacturer's specification (67).
Check/adjust tyre pressures, including spare (34).
Check tightness of road wheel fastenings (32).
Check condition and security of steering unit, joints and gaiters.
Check security of suspension fixings.
Check steering and suspension for oil/fluid leaks.
Inspect brake pads for wear, discs for condition (35).
Check brake servo hoses/pipe for security.
Check/adjust foot and hand brake (35).
Check visually hydraulic pipes and unions for chafing, leaks and corrosion.
Check/adjust front wheel alignment.
Check output of charging system.
Check function of original equipment, i.e. interior and exterior lamps, horns, warning indicators, windscreen wipers and washers.
Check, if necessary renew, wiper blades (46).
Check/adjust headlamp alignment.
Check instrumentation.
Check condition and security of seats, seat belts and seat belt warning system.

Road test
Road/roller test and check operation of all instrumentation.
Report additional work required.

Brakes
It is further recommended that at 19,000 miles (or 18 months) the brake fluid is renewed. This additional work should be carried out by your authorized Austin MG Dealer.

'D' SERVICE
Lubrication
Lubricate all grease points (excluding hubs) (78).
Renew engine oil and filter (50).
Check/top up brake fluid reservoir (37).
Check/top up clutch fluid reservoir (36)
Check/top up battery electrolyte (39).
Check/top up cooling system (30).
Check/top up gearbox and rear axle oils (63 and 64).
Check/top up screen washer reservoir (47).
†Lubricate distributor (48).
Lubricate accelerator control linkage and pedal pivot, check operation (78).
Lubricate all locks and hinges (not steering lock).

Maintenance Summary

Engine

†Check driving belts, adjust or renew (51 and 59).
 Check cooling system hoses/pipes for security and condition.
†Renew carburetter air cleaner element (61).
†Renew air pump air filter (59).
†Check gulp valve and check valve operation.
†Check air injection system hoses/pipes for security.
†Check air intake temperature control system.
†Check crankcase breathing and evaporative loss systems. Check hoses/pipes and restrictors for blockage, security and condition.
†Check/adjust valve clearances (52).
†Check exhaust system for leaks and security.

Ignition

†Check ignition wiring for fraying, chafing and deterioration.
†Renew spark plugs (49).
†Renew distributor points.
†Clean distributor cap; check for cracks and tracking (48).
†Check/adjust dwell angle and ignition timing, using electronic equipment.

Fuel system

†Renew fuel line filter (58).
†Check fuel system for leaks.
†Top up carburetter piston damper (62).
†Check/adjust carburetter idle settings.
†Check condition of fuel filler cap seal.

Safety

 Check tyres for tread depth, visually for cuts in tyre fabric, exposure of ply or cord structure, lumps and bulges.
 Check that tyres comply with manufacturer's specification (67).
 Check/adjust tyre pressures, including spare (34).
 Check tightness of road wheel fastenings (32).
 Check condition and security of steering unit, joints and gaiters.
 Check security of suspension fixings.
 Check steering and suspension for oil/fluid leaks.
 Inspect brake linings/pads for wear, drums/discs for condition (35 and 36).
 Check brake servo hoses/pipes for security.
 Check/adjust foot and hand brake (35).
 Check visually hydraulic pipes and unions for chafing, leaks and corrosion.
 Check/adjust front wheel alignment.
 Check output of charging system.
 Check function of original equipment, i.e. interior and exterior lamps, horns, warning indicators, windscreen wipers and washers.
 Check, if necessary renew, wiper blades (46).
 Check/adjust headlamp alignment.
 Check instrumentation.
 Check operation of all door locks and window controls.
 Check condition and security of seats, seat belts, and seat belt warning system.

Road test

Road/roller test and check operation of all instrumentation.
Report additional work required.

Brakes

It is further recommended that every 37,500 miles (or 3 years) the brake fluid, hydraulic seals and hoses in the brake and clutch hydraulic systems are renewed. Examine working surfaces of pistons and bores in master, slave, and wheel cylinders and renew parts as necessary. Renew brake servo filter. This additional work should be carried out by your authorized Austin MG Dealer.

'E' SERVICE

Lubrication

Lubricate all grease points (excluding hubs) (78).
Renew engine oil and filter (50).
Check/top up brake fluid reservoir (37).
Check/top up clutch fluid reservoir (36).
Check/top up battery electrolyte (39).
Check/top up cooling system (30).
Check/top up gearbox (non-overdrive) and rear axle oils (63 and 64).
Drain gearbox and overdrive, clean filters and refill with new oil (63).
Check/top up screen washer reservoir (47).
†Lubricate distributor (48).
† Lubricate accelerator control linkage and pedal pivot, check operation (78).
Lubricate all locks and hinges (not steering lock).

Engine

†Check driving belts; adjust or renew (51 and 59).
Check cooling system hoses/pipes for security and condition.
†Renew carburetter air cleaner element (61).
†Renew air pump air filter element (59).
†Check gulp valve and check valve operation.
†Check air injection system hoses/pipes for security.
†Check air intake temperature control system.
†Check crankcase breathing and evaporative loss systems. Check hoses/pipes and restrictors for blockage, security and condition.
†Check/adjust valve clearances (52).
†Check E.G.R. system.
†Renew adsorption canister (58).
†Check exhaust system for leaks and security.

Maintenance Summary

Ignition
†Check ignition wiring for fraying, chafing and deterioration.
†Renew spark plugs (49).
†Renew distributor points.
†Clean distributor cap; check for cracks and tracking (48).
†Check/adjust dwell angle and ignition timing using electronic equipment.

Fuel system
†Renew fuel line filter (58).
†Check fuel system for leaks.
†Top up carburetter piston damper (62).
†Check/adjust carburetter idle settings.
†Check condition of fuel filler cap seal (60).

Safety
Check tyres for tread depth, visually for cuts in tyre fabric, exposure of ply or cord structure, lumps and bulges.
Check that tyres comply with manufacturer's specification (67).
Check/adjust tyre pressures, including spare (34).
Check tightness of road wheel fastenings (32).
Check condition and security of steering unit, joints and gaiters.
Check security of suspension fixings.
Check steering and suspension for oil/fluid leaks.
Inspect brake linings/pads for wear, drum/discs for condition (35 and 36).
Check brake servo hoses/pipes for security.
Check/adjust front wheel alignment.
Check/adjust foot and hand brake (35).
Check visually hydraulic pipes and unions for chafing, leaks and corrosion.
Check output of charging system.
Check function of original equipment, i.e. interior and exterior lamps, horns, warning indicators, windscreen wipers and washers.
Check, if necessary renew, wiper blades (46).
Check/adjust headlamp alignment.
Check instrumentation.
Check operation of all door locks and window controls.
Check condition and security of seats, seat belts and seat belt warning system.

Road test
Road/roller test and check operation of all instrumentation.
Report additional work required.

LUBRICATION

The lubrication systems of your new car are filled with high quality oils. You should always use a high quality oil of the correct viscosity range in the engine, gearbox and rear axle during subsequent maintenance operations or when topping up. The use of oils not to the correct specification can lead to high oil and fuel consumption and ultimately do damage to the engine, gearbox or rear axle components.

Oils to the correct specification contain additives which disperse the corrosive acids formed by combustion and also prevent the formation of sludge which can block oilways. **Additional oil additives should not be used.** Servicing intervals must be adhered to.

Engine Use a well known brand of oil to B.L.S. O.L. O.R. or MIL-L-R104B or A.P.1, SE quality, with a viscosity band spanning the temperature range of your locality.

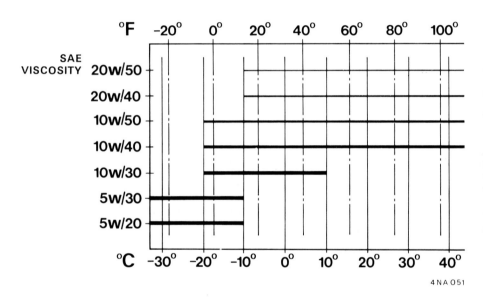

4NA051

Synchromesh gearbox Use the same oil selected for the engine.

Rear axle and steering rack Top up and refill with H.D.90 (MIL-L-2105B) above −10°C (10°F) or H.D.80 (MIL-L-2105B) below −5°C (20°F).

Grease points Use Multipurpose Lithium Grease N.L.G.1 consistency No. 2.

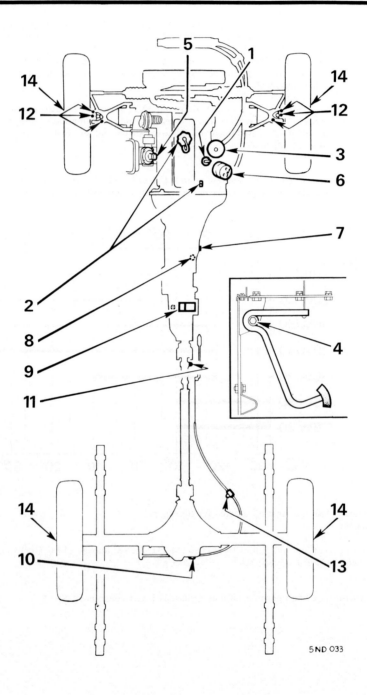

5 ND 033

NOTE: Ensure that the vehicle is standing on a level surface when checking the oil levels.

WEEKLY
   (1)   ENGINE. Check oil level, and top up if necessary.

'A' SERVICE
   (2)   ENGINE. Drain and refill with new oil.
   (4)   THROTTLE. Lubricate throttle control linkage, cable and accelerator pedal fulcrum.
   (5)   CARBURETTER. Top up carburetter piston damper.
   (6)   DISTRIBUTOR. Lubricate all parts as necessary.
   (8)   GEARBOX (NON OVERDRIVE). Drain and refill with new oil.
   (9)   GEARBOX WITH OVERDRIVE. Drain, clean overdrive filters, refill with new oil—refer to page 63.
  (10)   REAR AXLE. Check oil level, and top up if necessary.
  (11)   PROPELLER SHAFT (1 nipple)   ⎫
  (12)   FRONT SUSPENSION (6 nipples)   ⎬ Give three or four strokes with a grease gun.
  (13)   HAND BRAKE CABLE (1 nipple)   ⎭
  (14)   WIRE WHEELS. Lubricate wire wheel and hub splines.
         LOCKS, HINGES AND LINKAGES. Lubricate all door, bonnet, boot locks and hinges (not steering lock), and hand brake mechanical linkage.
         FRICTION POINTS. Spray lubricant on all friction points.

'B' SERVICE
   (1)   ENGINE. Check oil level, and top up if necessary.
   (7)   GEARBOX. Check oil level, and top up if necessary.
  (10)   REAR AXLE. Check oil level, and top up if necessary.
  (11)   PROPELLER SHAFT (1 nipple)   ⎫
  (12)   FRONT SUSPENSION (6 nipples)   ⎬ Give three or four strokes with a grease gun.
  (13)   HAND BRAKE CABLE (1 nipple)   ⎭
  (14)   WIRE WHEELS ONLY. Grease wheel and hub splines.
         FRICTION POINTS. Spray lubricant on all friction points.

'C' AND 'D' SERVICES
   (2)   ENGINE. Drain and refill with new oil.
   (3)   ENGINE OIL FILTER. Remove disposable cartridge; fit new.
   (4)   THROTTLE. Lubricate throttle control linkage, cable and accelerator pedal fulcrum.
   (5)   CARBURETTER. Top up carburetter piston damper—'D' SERVICE only.
   (6)   DISTRIBUTOR. Lubricate all parts as necessary.
   (7)   GEARBOX. Check oil level, and top up if necessary.
  (10)   REAR AXLE. Check oil level, and top up if necessary.
  (11)   PROPELLER SHAFT (1 nipple)   ⎫
  (12)   FRONT SUSPENSION (6 nipples)   ⎬ Give three or four strokes with a grease gun.
  (13)   HAND BRAKE CABLE (1 nipple)   ⎭
  (14)   WIRE WHEELS ONLY. Grease wheel and hub splines.
         LOCKS, HINGES AND LINKAGES. Lubricate all door, bonnet, boot locks and hinges (not steering lock); and the hand brake mechanical linkage.
         FRICTION POINTS. Spray lubricant on all friction points.

'E' SERVICE
Carry out a 'D' SERVICE in addition to the following:
   (9)   GEARBOX WITH OVERDRIVE. Drain, clean overdrive filters, refill with new oil—refer to page 63.

MGB
TOURER (GHN 5UF)

Driver's Handbook Supplement

To be used with Handbook AKM 3286

CATALYTIC CONVERTER EQUIPPED CARS

© BRITISH LEYLAND UK LIMITED 1975

WARNING SYSTEMS

Catalytic converter and exhaust gas recirculation (E.G.R.) valve
Fig. 1

The warning lamp (1) for the catalytic converter and E.G.R. valve will glow when the car has completed a service interval mileage of approximately 25,000 miles, indicating that the E.G.R. valve should be serviced and the catalytic converter renewed. It is recommended that this work is carried out by an authorized Austin MG Dealer. An E.G.R. emission service repair kit and a catalytic converter together with a service interval reset key can be purchased from an authorized Austin MG Dealer.

Complete details in servicing the E.G.R. valve and renewing the catalytic converter are given in Workshop Manual Part No. AKM 3297 obtainable from authorized Austin MG Dealers.

NOTE: As an automatic check the warning lamp will glow each time the ignition key is turned to position **'III'** (starter motor operating). Consult your authorized Austin MG Dealer if the lamp fails to glow when the starter is operated.

Catalytic converter and E.G.R. valve service interval counter
Fig. 1

The service interval counter (2) for the catalytic converter and the E.G.R. valve is located in the engine compartment and indicates the percentage of service interval mileage that has been completed in a 25,000 mile period.

The counter should be reset to zero immediately after the E.G.R. valve has been serviced and the catalytic converter renewed.

Fig. 1

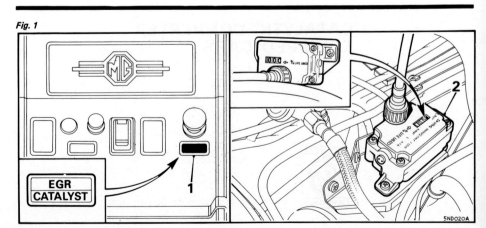

RUNNING INSTRUCTIONS

Exhaust catalytic converter

The catalytic converter is fitted into the exhaust system in order to reduce carbon monoxide and hydrocarbon emissions.

On completion of each 25,000 miles the necessity for renewal of the catalytic converter will be indicated by the catalytic converter warning light glowing.

1. The catalytic converter contains ceramic material. Avoid heavy impacts on the converter casing.
2. **Use unleaded fuel only.** The use of leaded fuel will seriously impair the efficiency of the emission control system.
3. The reaction in the catalytic converter increases exhaust system temperatures. Care must be taken to avoid exhaust system contact with easily combustible materials such as dry grass.
4. If the engine misfires, the cause must be immediately rectified to prevent catalytic converter damage.
5. The use of any device which requires an insert into a spark plug hole in order to generate an air pressure, i.e. tyre pump or paint spray attachment, could also result in catalytic converter damage.

Choice of fuel

The engine fitted with a catalytic converter is designed to operate only on unleaded fuel. It is essential that **unleaded fuel is used** otherwise serious damage can be caused in the catalytic converter.

Filling with fuel

The filler neck of the fuel tank is designed to accept fuel dispenser nozzles of the type specified only for unleaded fuel.

IGNITION

Ignition timing The ignition timing is set dynamically to give optimum engine performance with efficient engine emission control. Electronic test equipment must be used to check the ignition timing setting and the automatic advance (see **'GENERAL DATA'**). Checking and adjustment to the ignition timing setting should be carried out by your authorized Austin MG Dealer.

Basic tuning data will be found on the Vehicle Emission Control Information Label located in the engine compartment.

Distributor
Fig. 1 Release the retaining clips and remove the cover (1). Remove the rotor arm (2) and the anti-flash shield (3).

Lubrication. Add a few drops of oil to the felt pad (4) in the top of the timing rotor carrier.

Remove the anti-flash shield and lubricate the pick-up plate centre bearing with a drop of oil in each of the two holes (5) in the base plate.

Apply a few drops of oil through the aperture (6) to lubricate the centrifugal timing control.

Cleaning. With a clean nap-free cloth wipe the inside of the distributor cover, the rotor arm and the anti-flash shield. Refit the anti-flash shield, ensuring that the cut-outs are aligned with the distributor cover retaining clips. Refit the rotor arm and the cover.

Fig. 1

4ND311A

GENERAL DATA

Engine

Type	18V 801AE Standard	
	18V 802AE Overdrive	
Bore	3·16 in	80·26 mm
Stroke	3·5 in	89 mm
No. of cylinders	4	
Capacity	110 in³	1800 cc
Compressed ratio	8 : 1	
Firing order	1, 3, 4, 2	
Valve clearance—set warm	0·013 in	0·33 mm
Oil pressure: Idling	10 to 25 lbf/in²	0·17 to 1·7 kgf/cm²
Normal	50 to 80 lbf/in²	3·5 to 5·6 kgf/cm²
Idle speed	850 rev/min	
Exhaust gas content analyser reading		
at idle speed	$5\frac{1}{2} \pm 1\%$ CO maximum	

Ignition

Stroboscopic ignition timing ..	10° B.T.D.C. at 1500 rev/min	
Timing marks	Notch on crankshaft pulley, pointers on timing chain cover	
Sparking plugs	Champion N-9Y	
Plug gap	0·035 in	0·90 mm

MAINTENANCE SUMMARY

Basic engine tuning data will be found on the Vehicle Emission Control Information label located in the engine compartment.

Detailed maintenance instructions will be found on the page indicated after each item in the Handbook.

The following items should be checked weekly by the driver:
Engine oil level (50)
Brake fluid level (37)
Radiator coolant level (30)
Battery electrolyte level (39)
Windshield washer reservoir fluid level (47)
All tyre pressures (34)
All lights for operation
Horn operation
Windshield wipers operation

MAINTENANCE LEVELS

† **These items are emission related**

Service	Mileage × 1000	Monthly intervals	Page No.
A	1	After Sales Service	70
B	3, 9, 16, 22, 28, 34, 41, 47	3	71
C	6, 19, 31, 44	6	72
D	12·5, 37·5	12	73
E	25, 50	24	75

NOTE: The service intervals are based on an annual mileage of approximately 12,500 miles. Should the vehicle complete substantially less miles than this per annum, it is recommended that a 'C' service is completed at six-month intervals, and a 'D' service at twelve-month intervals.

'A' SERVICE
Lubrication
Lubricate all grease points (excluding hubs).
Renew engine oil (50).
Check/top up brake fluid reservoir (37).
Check/top up clutch fluid reservoir (36).
Check/top up battery electrolyte (39).
Check/top up cooling system (30).
Check/top up rear axle (64).
Drain gearbox, refill with new oil (non overdrive) (63).
Drain gearbox and overdrive, clean filters and refill with new oil (63).
Check/top up screen washer reservoir (47).
†Lubricate distributor (Supplement page 4).
†Lubricate accelerator control linkage and pedal pivot; check operation (78).
Lubricate all locks and hinges (not steering lock).

Engine
†Check driving belts; adjust or renew (51 and 59).
Check cooling system hoses/pipes for security and condition.
†Check crankcase breathing and evaporative loss system. Check hoses/pipes for security.
†Check air injection system hoses/pipes for security.
†Check security of engine bolts and mountings.
†Check/adjust torque of cylinder head nuts.
†Check/adjust valve clearance (52).
†Check security of E.G.R. valve operating lines.
†Check exhaust system for leaks and security.

'A' SERVICE—*continued*

Ignition
†Check ignition wiring for fraying, chafing and deterioration.
†Check/adjust ignition timing, using electronic equipment.

Fuel system
†Check fuel system for leaks.
†Top up carburetter piston damper (62).
†Check/adjust carburetter idle settings.

Safety
Check tyres for tread depth, visually for cuts in tyre fabric, exposure of ply and cord structure lumps and bulges.
Check/adjust tyre pressures, including spare (34).
Check tightness of road wheel fastenings (32).
Check condition and security of steering unit, joints and gaiters.
Check security of suspension fixings.
Check steering and suspension for oil/fluid leaks.
Check brake servo hoses/pipes for security.
Check/adjust foot and hand brake (35).
Check visually hydraulic pipes and unions for chafing, leaks and corrosion.
Check/adjust front wheel alignment.
Check output of charging system.
Check function of original equipment, i.e. interior and exterior lamps, horns, warning indicators, windscreen wipers and washers.
Check/adjust headlamp alignment.
Check instrumentation.
Check operation of all door locks and window controls.

Road test
Road/roller test and check operation of all instrumentation.
Report additional work required.

'B' SERVICE

Lubrication
Lubricate all grease points (excluding hubs) (78).
Check/top up engine oil (50).
Check/top up brake fluid reservoir (37).
Check/top up clutch fluid reservoir (36).
Check/top up battery electrolyte (39).
Check/top up cooling system (30).
Check/top up gearbox and rear axle oils (63 and 64).
Check/top up screen washer reservoir (47).

Engine
†Check fan drive belt; adjust or renew (51).
†Check exhaust system for leaks and security.

Maintenance Summary

'B' SERVICE—*continued*

Fuel system
  †Check fuel system for leaks.

Safety
  Check tyres for tread depth, visually for cuts in tyre fabric, exposure of ply or cord structure, lumps or bulges.
  Check that tyres comply with manufacturer's specification (67).
  Check/adjust tyre pressures, including spare (34).
  Check tightness of road wheel fastenings (32).
  Check condition and security of steering unit, joints and gaiters.
  Check steering and suspension for oil/fluid leaks.
  Check/adjust foot and hand brake (35).
  Check visually hydraulic pipes and unions for chafing, leaks and corrosion.
  Check function of original equipment, i.e. interior and exterior lamps, horns, warning indicators, windscreen wipers and washers.
  Check, if necessary renew, wiper blades (46).
  Check/adjust headlamp alignment.

'C' SERVICE

Lubrication
  Lubricate all grease points (excluding hubs) (78).
  Renew engine oil and filter (50).
  Check/top up brake fluid reservoir (37).
  Check/top up clutch fluid reservoir (36).
  Check/top up battery electrolyte (39).
  Check/top up cooling system (30).
  Check/top up gearbox and rear axle oils (63 and 64).
  Check/top up screen washer reservoir (47).
  †Lubricate distributor (Supplement page 4).
  †Lubricate accelerator control linkage and pedal pivot; check operation (78).
  Lubricate all locks and hinges (not steering lock).

Engine
  †Check fan drive belt; adjust or renew (51).
  Check cooling system hoses/pipes for security and condition.
  †Check exhaust system for leaks and security.

Ignition
  †Clean spark plugs (49).

Fuel system
  †Check fuel system for leaks.

'C' SERVICE—*continued*

Safety
Check tyres for tread depth, visually for cuts in tyre fabric, exposure of ply or cord structure, lumps and bulges.
Check that tyres comply with manufacturer's specification (67).
Check/adjust tyre pressures, including spare (34).
Check tightness of road wheel fastenings (32).
Check condition and security of steering unit, joints and gaiters.
Check security of suspension fixings.
Check steering and suspension for oil/fluid leaks.
Inspect brake pads for wear, discs for condition (35).
Check brake servo hoses/pipe for security.
Check/adjust foot and hand brake (35).
Check visually hydraulic pipes and unions for chafing, leaks and corrosion.
Check/adjust front wheel alignment.
Check output of charging system.
Check function of original equipment, i.e. interior and exterior lamps, horns, warning indicators, windscreen wipers and washers.
Check, if necessary renew, wiper blades (46).
Check/adjust headlamp alignment.
Check instrumentation.
Check condition and security of seats, seat belts and seat belt warning system.

Road test
Road/roller test and check operation of all instrumentation.
Report additional work required.

Brakes
It is further recommended that at 19,000 miles (or 18 months) the brake fluid is renewed. This additional work should be carried out by your authorized Austin MG Dealer.

'D' SERVICE

Lubrication
Lubricate all grease points (excluding hubs) (78).
Renew engine oil and filter (50).
Check/top up brake fluid reservoir (37).
Check/top up clutch fluid reservoir (36).
Check/top up battery electrolyte (39).
Check/top up cooling system (30).
Check/top up gearbox and rear axle oils (63 and 64).
Check/top up screen washer reservoir (47).
†Lubricate distributor (Supplement page 4).
Lubricate accelerator control linkage and pedal pivot, check operation (78).
Lubricate all locks and hinges (not steering lock).

Maintenance Summary

'D' SERVICE—*continued*

Engine
†Check driving belts, adjust or renew (51 and 59).
 Check cooling system hoses/pipes for security and condition.
†Renew carburetter air cleaner element (61).
†Renew air pump air filter (59).
†Check gulp valve and check valve operation.
†Check air injection system hoses/pipes for security.
†Check air intake temperature control system.
†Check crankcase breathing and evaporative loss systems. Check hoses/pipes and restrictors for blockage, security and condition.
†Check/adjust valve clearances (52).
†Check exhaust system for leaks and security.

Ignition
†Check ignition wiring for fraying, chafing and deterioration.
†Renew spark plugs (49).
†Clean distributor cap; check for cracks and tracking (48).
†Check/adjust ignition timing, using electronic equipment.

Fuel system
†Renew fuel line filter (58).
†Check fuel system for leaks.
†Top up carburetter piston damper (62).
†Check/adjust carburetter idle settings.
†Check condition of fuel filler cap seal.

Safety
 Check tyres for tread depth, visually for cuts in tyre fabric, exposure of ply or cord structure, lumps and bulges.
 Check that tyres comply with manufacturer's specification (67).
 Check/adjust tyre pressures, including spare (34).
 Check tightness of road wheel fastenings (32).
 Check condition and security of steering unit, joints and gaiters.
 Check security of suspension fixings.
 Check steering and suspension for oil/fluid leaks.
 Inspect brake linings/pads for wear, drums/discs for condition (35 and 36).
 Check brake servo hoses/pipes for security.
 Check/adjust foot and hand brake (35).
 Check visually hydraulic pipes and unions for chafing, leaks and corrosion.
 Check/adjust front wheel alignment.
 Check output of charging system.
 Check function of original equipment, i.e. interior and exterior lamps, horns, warning indicators, windscreen wipers and washers.
 Check, if necessary renew, wiper blades (46).
 Check/adjust headlamp alignment.
 Check instrumentation.
 Check operation of all door locks and window controls.
 Check condition and security of seats, seat belts, and seat belt warning system.

'D' SERVICE—*continued*

Road test
Road/roller test and check operation of all instrumentation.
Report additional work required.

Brakes
It is further recommended that every 37,500 miles (or 3 years) the brake fluid, hydraulic seals and hoses in the brake and clutch hydraulic systems are renewed. Examine working surfaces of pistons and bores in master, slave, and wheel cylinders and renew parts as necessary. Renew brake servo filter. This additional work should be carried out by your authorized Austin MG Dealer.

'E' SERVICE

Lubrication
Lubricate all grease points (excluding hubs) (78).
Renew engine oil and filter (50).
Check/top up brake fluid reservoir (37).
Check/top up clutch fluid reservoir (36).
Check/top up battery electrolyte (39).
Check/top up cooling system (30).
Check/top up gearbox (non-overdrive) and rear axle oils (63 and 64).
Drain gearbox and overdrive, clean filters and refill with new oil (63).
Check/top up screen washer reservoir (47).
†Lubricate distributor (Supplement page 4).
†Lubricate accelerator control linkage and pedal pivot, check operation (78).
Lubricate all locks and hinges (not steering lock).

Engine
†Check driving belts; adjust or renew (51 and 59).
Check cooling system hoses/pipes for security and condition.
†Renew carburetter air cleaner element (61).
†Renew air pump air filter element (59).
†Check gulp valve and check valve operation.
†Check air injection system hoses/pipes for security.
†Check air intake temperature control system.
†Check crankcase breathing and evaporative loss systems. Check hoses/pipes and restrictors for blockage, security and condition.
†Check/adjust valve clearances (52).
†Check E.G.R. system.
†Renew catalytic converter.
†Renew absorption canister (58).
†Check exhaust system for leaks and security.

Ignition
†Check ignition wiring for fraying, chafing and deterioration.
†Renew spark plugs (49).
†Clean distributor cap; check for cracks and tracking (48).
†Check/adjust ignition timing using electronic equipment.

Maintenance Summary

'E' SERVICE—*continued*

Fuel system
†Renew fuel line filter (58).
†Check fuel system for leaks.
†Top up carburetter piston damper (62).
†Check/adjust carburetter idle settings.
†Check condition of fuel filler cap seal (60).

Safety
Check tyres for tread depth, visually for cuts in tyre fabric, exposure of ply or cord structure, lumps and bulges.
Check that tyres comply with manufacturer's specification (67).
Check/adjust tyre pressures, including spare (34).
Check tightness of road wheel fastenings (32).
Check condition and security of steering unit, joints and gaiters.
Check security of suspension fixings.
Check steering and suspension for oil/fluid leaks.
Inspect brake linings/pads for wear, drum/discs for condition (35 and 36).
Check brake servo hoses/pipes for security.
Check/adjust front wheel alignment.
Check/adjust foot and hand brake (35).
Check visually hydraulic pipes and unions for chafing, leaks and corrosion.
Check output of charging system.
Check function of original equipment, i.e. interior and exterior lamps, horns, warning indicators, windscreen wipers and washers.
Check, if necessary renew, wiper blades (46).
Check/adjust headlamp alignment.
Check instrumentation.
Check operation of all door locks and window controls.
Check condition and security of seats, seat belts and seat belt warning system.

Road test
Road/roller test and check operation of all instrumentation.
Report additional work required.

NOTES

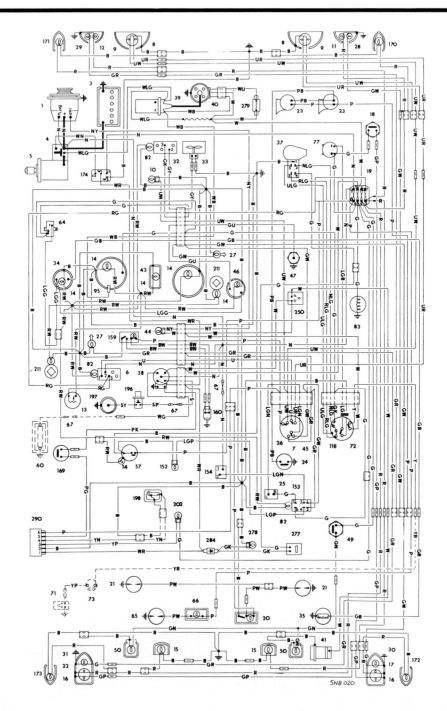

5NB 020

KEY TO THE WIRING DIAGRAM

1. Alternator
3. Battery
4. Starter solenoid
5. Starter motor
6. Lighting switch
7. Headlamp dip switch
8. Headlamp dip beam
9. Headlamp main beam
10. Headlamp main beam warning lamp
11. R.H. parking lamp
12. L.H. parking lamp
13. Panel lamp rheostat switch
14. Panel illumination lamp
15. Number-plate illumination lamp
16. Stop lamp
17. R.H. tail lamp
18. Stop lamp switch
19. Fuse unit (4-way)
20. Interior courtesy lamp
21. Interior lamp door switch
22. L.H. tail lamp
23. Horn
24. Horn-push
25. Flasher unit
26. Direction indicator switch
27. Direction indicator warning lamp
28. R.H. front direction indicator lamp
29. L.H. front direction indicator lamp
30. R.H. rear direction indicator lamp
31. L.H. rear direction indicator lamp
32. Heater motor switch
33. Heater motor
34. Fuel gauge.
35. Fuel gauge tank unit
37. Windscreen wiper motor
38. Ignition/starter switch
39. Ignition coil
40. Distributor
41. Fuel pump
43. Oil pressure gauge
44. Ignition warning lamp
45. Headlamp flasher switch

46. Coolant temperature gauge
47. Coolant temperature transmitter
49. Reverse lamp switch
50. Reverse lamp
57. Cigar lighter
60. Radio*
64. Instrument voltage stabilizer
65. Luggage compartment lamp switch
66. Luggage compartment lamp
67. Line fuse
71. Overdrive solenoid*
72. Overdrive manual control switch*
73. Overdrive gear switch*
77. Windscreen washer pump
82. Switch illumination lamp
83. Induction heater
95. Tachometer
118. Combined windscreen washer and wiper switch
152. Hazard warning lamp
153. Hazard warning switch
154. Hazard warning flasher unit
159. Brake pressure warning lamp and lamp test-push
160. Brake pressure failure switch
169. Ignition key audible warning door switch
170. R.H. front side-marker lamp
171. L.H. front side-marker lamp
172. R.H. rear side-marker lamp
173. L.H. rear side-marker lamp
174. Starter solenoid relay
196. Running-on control valve
197. Running-on control valve oil pressure switch
198. Driver's seat belt buckle switch
202. 'Fasten belts' warning light
211. Heater control illumination lamp
250. Inertia switch
277. Service interval counter
278. Service interval counter warning lamp
279. Resistor—distributor
284. Diode for service interval counter
290. Time delay buzzer

* Optional fitment circuits shown dotted.

CABLE COLOUR CODE

N.	Brown.	P.	Purple.	W.	White.	K.	Pink.
U.	Blue.	G.	Green.	Y.	Yellow.	O.	Orange.
R.	Red.	LG.	Light Green	B.	Black.	S.	Slate.

When a cable has two colour code letters the first denotes the main
colour and the second denotes the tracer colour.

WIRING DIAGRAM (with sequential seat belt control)

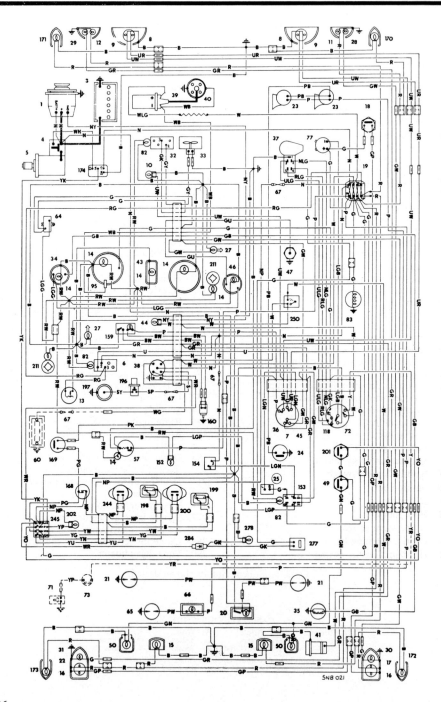

5NB 021

KEY TO THE WIRING DIAGRAM

1. Alternator
3. Battery
4. Starter solenoid
5. Starter motor
6. Lighting switch
7. Headlamp dip switch
8. Headlamp dip beam
9. Headlamp main beam
10. Headlamp main beam warning lamp
11. R.H. parking lamp
12. L.H. parking lamp
13. Panel lamp rheostat switch
14. Panel illumination lamp
15. Number-plate illumination lamp
16. Stop lamp
17. R.H. tail lamp
18. Stop lamp switch
19. Fuse unit (4-way)
20. Interior courtesy lamp
21. Interior lamp door switch
22. L.H. tail lamp
23. Horn
24. Horn-push
25. Flasher unit
26. Direction indicator switch
27. Direction indicator warning lamp
28. R.H. front direction indicator lamp
29. L.H. front direction indicator lamp
30. R.H. rear direction indicator lamp
31. L.H. rear direction indicator lamp
32. Heater motor switch
33. Heater motor
34. Fuel gauge
35. Fuel gauge tank unit
37. Windscreen wiper motor
38. Ignition/statrer switch
39. Ignition coil
40. Distributor
41. Fuel pump
43. Oil pressure gauge
44. Ignition warning lamp
45. Headlamp flasher switch
46. Coolant temperature gauge
47. Coolant temperature transmitter

49. Reverse lamp switch
50. Reverse lamp
57. Cigar lighter—illuminated
60. Radio*
64. Instrument voltage stabilizer
65. Luggage compartment lamp switch
66. Luggage compartment lamp
67. Line fuse
71. Overdrive solenoid*
72. Overdrive manual control switch*
73. Overdrive gear switch*
77. Windscreen washer pump
82. Switch illumination lamp
83. Induction heater
95. Tachometer
118. Combined windscreen washer and wiper switch
152. Hazard warning lamp
153. Hazard warning switch
154. Hazard warning flasher unit
159. Brake pressure warning lamp and lamp test-push
160. Brake pressure failure switch
168. Audible warning buzzer
169. Ignition key audible warning door switch
170. R.H. front side-marker lamp
171. L.H. front side-marker lamp
172. R.H. rear side-marker lamp
173. L.H. rear side-marker lamp
174. Starter solenoid relay
196. Running-on control valve
197. Running-on control valve oil pressure switch
198. Driver's seat belt buckle switch
199. Passenger's seat belt buckle switch
200. Passenger seat switch
201. Seat belt warning gearbox switch
202. 'Fasten belts' warning light
211. Heater control illumination lamp
244. Driver's seat switch
245. Sequential seat belt control unit
250. Inertia switch
277. Service interval counter
278. Service interval counter warning lamp
284. Diode for service interval counter

* Optional fitment circuits shown dotted

CABLE COLOUR CODE

N.	Brown	P.	Purple	W.	White	K.	Pink
U.	Blue	G.	Green	Y.	Yellow	O.	Orange
R.	Red	LG.	Light Green	B.	Black	S.	Slate

When a cable has two colour code letters the first denotes the main colour and the second denotes the tracer colour.

WIRING DIAGRAM (with limited period warning)

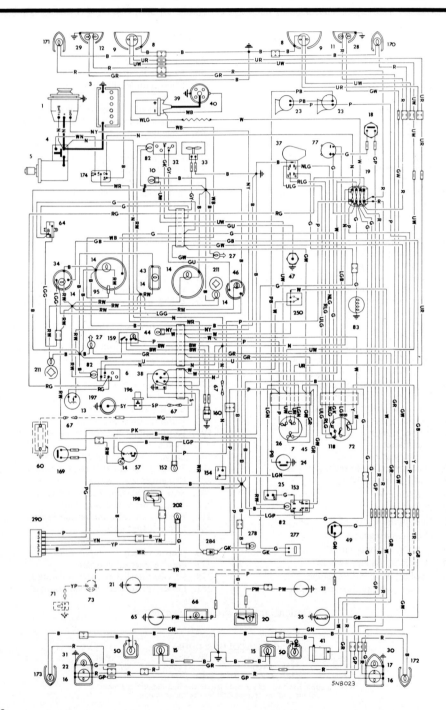

5NB023

KEY TO THE WIRING DIAGRAM

1. Alternator
3. Battery
4. Starter solenoid
5. Starter motor
6. Lighting switch
7. Headlamp dip switch
8. Headlamp dip beam
9. Headlamp main beam
10. Headlamp main beam warning lamp
11. R.H. parking lamp
12. L.H. parking lamp
13. Panel lamp rheostat switch
14. Panel illumination lamp
15. Number-plate illumination lamp
16. Stop lamp
17. R.H. tail lamp
18. Stop lamp switch
19. Fuse unit (4-way)
20. Interior courtesy lamp
21. Interior lamp door switch
22. L.H. tail lamp
23. Horn
24. Horn-push
25. Flasher unit
26. Direction indicator switch
27. Direction indicator warning lamp
28. R.H. front direction indicator lamp
29. L.H. front direction indicator lamp
30. R.H. rear direction indicator lamp
31. L.H. rear direction indicator lamp
32. Heater motor switch
33. Heater motor
34. Fuel gauge
35. Fuel gauge tank unit
37. Windscreen wiper motor
38. Ignition/starter switch
39. Ignition coil
40. Distributor
41. Fuel pump
43. Oil pressure gauge
44. Ignition warning lamp
45. Headlamp flasher switch
46. Coolant temperature gauge

47. Coolant temperature transmitter
49. Reverse lamp switch
50. Reverse lamp
57. Cigar lighter—illuminated
60. Radio*
64. Instrument voltage stabilizer
65. Luggage compartment lamp switch
66. Luggage compartment lamp
67. Line fuse
71. Overdrive solenoid*
72. Overdrive manual control switch*
73. Overdrive gear switch*
77. Windscreen washer pump
82. Switch illumination lamp
83. Induction heater
95. Tachometer
118. Combined windscreen washer and wiper switch
152. Hazard warning lamp
153. Hazard warning switch
154. Hazard warning flasher unit
159. Brake pressure warning lamp and lamp test-push
160. Brake pressure failure switch
168. Audible warning buzzer
169. Ignition key audible warning door switch
170. R.H. front side-marker lamp
171. L.H. front side-marker lamp
172. R.H. rear side-marker lamp
173. L.H. rear side-marker lamp
174. Starter solenoid relay
196. Running-on control valve
197. Running-on control valve oil pressure switch
198. Driver's seat belt buckle switch
202. 'Fasten belts' warning light
211. Heater control illumination lamp
250. Inertia switch
277. Service interval counter
278. Service interval counter warning lamp
284. Diode for service interval counter
290. Time delay buzzer

* Optional fitment circuits shown dotted

CABLE COLOUR CODE

N.	Brown	P.	Purple	W.	White	K.	Pink
U.	Blue	G.	Green	Y.	Yellow	O.	Orange
R.	Red	LG.	Light Green	B.	Black	S.	Slate

When a cable has two colour code letters the first denotes the main colour and the second denotes the tracer colour.

© Copyright British Leyland Motor Corporation 1975
and Brooklands Books Limited 1995

This book is published by Brooklands Books Limited and based upon text and
illustrations protected by copyright and first published in 1975 by British Leyland
Motor Corporation and may not be reproduced transmitted or copied by any means
without the prior written permission of Rover Group Limited and
Brooklands Books Limited.

Printed and distributed by Brooklands Books Ltd., PO Box 146, Cobham,
Surrey KT11 1LG, England Phone: 01932 865051 Fax: 01932 868803
E-mail: sales@brooklands-books.com   www.brooklands-books.com

Part Number: AKM 3286 MGB (USA) including supplements
AKM 3413 MGB (USA & Canada) and AKM 3404 MGB (USA)

ISBN 1 870642 546   Ref: B-MG799HH   15/4Z1